IMAGES
of America

DRUID HILLS

For John
with best regards.

Jennie Richardson

This *Atlanta Centennial Year Book* cover shows several elements that were important to the founding of Atlanta: a log cabin, a Native American, a pioneer, signs for Rich's and Muse's stores and skyscrapers in the background. It does not, however, indicate that Atlanta was a railroad hub (in fact, the city's first name was Terminus) or that General Sherman burned the city to the ground during the Civil War. (Personal collection of Jennifer J. Richardson.)

ON THE COVER: A garden party for employees of Cator Woolford's Retail Credit Company is held on the southern end of the formal gardens at Woolford's Jacqueland estate in Druid Hills. Couples dance to music from a live orchestra on an outdoor stage while the estate's mansion peeks over the trees. (Courtesy of Cator Sparks, great-grandson of Cator Woolford.)

IMAGES
of America

DRUID HILLS

Jennifer J. Richardson and Sue Sullivan

ARCADIA
PUBLISHING

Published by Arcadia Publishing
Charleston, South Carolina

Printed in the United States of America

Library of Congress Control Number: 2019931230

For all general information, please contact Arcadia Publishing:
Telephone 843-853-2070
Fax 843-853-0044
E-mail sales@arcadiapublishing.com
For customer service and orders:
Toll-Free 1-888-313-2665

Visit us on the Internet at www.arcadiapublishing.com

*For our heroes, Olmsted scholars Sally Harbaugh and Dr. Dana White;
the Druid Hills Civic Association; the Olmsted Linear Park Alliance;
Dr. Allan Williams; Alan Wayne Richardson;
and the community we love*

CONTENTS

Foreword   6

Acknowledgments   7

Introduction   8

1.   Druid Hills Is Born   11

2.   The First Family of Druid Hills   15

3.   Rich and Influential Citizens Build in Druid Hills   31

4.   Expansion in the 1920s–1960s   55

5.   Schools, Parks, and Churches   75

6.   Businesses, Institutions, and Organizations   89

7.   The Decline of Druid Hills   107

8.   Druid Hills Fights an Expressway   121

Druid Hills Today   127

FOREWORD

Frederick Law Olmsted believed that a city is a living organism and that urban parks are the necessary lungs of the healthy urban *corpus*. Druid Hills, Olmsted's last major executed work of community development, is a coordinated ensemble of byways and paths, of copses and linear parks, and of skillfully planned and well-crafted homes carefully sited within designed landscapes that were intended to look as though they were not designed at all. The scenographic picture here is adorned by a natural topography, by native plants and trees, and by regional species of flora and fauna that perennially renew the joie de vivre of the inhabitants of the Druid Hills community. Olmsted's realization of nature and man in harmony with beauty and art is an ideal balance of sustainability and compatibility, in which traditional values and modern life coexist in a holistic totality.

Jennifer Richardson is a keen observer of more than a century of Druid Hills history and development, writing about the owners and architects of Druid Hills houses, as well as the custodians and sometimes abusers of Olmsted's vision. She has celebrated successes when preservationists, sensitive architects, and educated property owners demonstrate their understanding of Olmsted's concepts, and when they collaborate to maintain compatibility and integrity of place in their interventions in the neighborhood. She has decried urban planners, developers, and civic leaders too ready to compromise a community masterpiece that previous generations have guarded so responsibly. She cares deeply about this place. Sue Sullivan's appreciation of homes and their histories and her devotion to the community caused her to seek out the stories of residents of Druid Hills and to record it—as if these homes could speak. Her desire is to keep the history of Druid Hills alive.

Ultimately, the naturalness and utter rightness of Druid Hills as an Olmsted environment is sensed and felt more easily than objectified and described. In writing about art, it is always the intangible spirit that eludes description through word or image. Architect Christopher Alexander may well have captured the essence of that elusive quality of environmental art in his 1979 book *The Timeless Way of Building* when he referenced "the quality without a name." In the end, Druid Hills adds up to more than a sum of its definable parts; its sense of place is quintessentially and ultimately defined by the quality without a name.

Robert M. Craig

ACKNOWLEDGMENTS

Many individuals and groups helped make this book a reality. We are grateful to the board of directors and individual members of the Druid Hills Civic Association and the members of the Landmark District Preservation Committee, who have been the key sponsors and cheerleaders for this effort. We appreciate the support of the board of the Olmsted Linear Park Alliance. We are grateful to the DeKalb History Center and historian Ken Thomas, board member. A special thank-you goes to the Stuart A. Rose Manuscript, Archives, and Rare Book Library at Emory University and all the wonderful staff who assisted us. We are eternally grateful to the many Druid Hills residents who shared documents, photographs, and stories, without which this book would not be possible.

Sue Sullivan especially thanks the many friends whom she's met while collecting these stories and photographs in her quest to keep the history of Druid Hills preserved. These people have enriched her life immeasurably. The coauthors, who did now know each other before commencing the project, also share a bond of new friendship and ongoing fascination with uncovering the history and mysteries in Druid Hills. We currently have more history than this book allows and are continuing to uncover more as part of our ongoing effort.

Special gratitude goes to Jennie's husband, Wayne Richardson, who supported Sue and Jennie in every endeavor and understands the mysteries of computers. Jennie is thankful for the valuable lessons passed on by her grandparents A.B. and Melba Mitcham and her brother Dr. Allan T. Williams, who taught her to love and revere history, preserve everything, and never throw anything away.

Both Jennie and Sue send thanks to Angel Hisnanick and David Mandel, our contacts and editors at Arcadia, for their patience, good humor, and expertise.

Unless otherwise noted, all images appear courtesy of the collection of Jennifer J. Richardson.

INTRODUCTION

Prior to the arrival of white settlers in Georgia, Creek and Cherokee Tribes inhabited land now within Druid Hills. With abundant creeks and fertile bottom land, it was an ideal place for Native Americans to live. In 1821, the land that is now Druid Hills was ceded by Native Americans to Georgia. In 1830, the Indian Removal Act resulted in most Native Americans leaving Georgia on the Trail of Tears, and their former land was given to whites by lottery.

On April 12, 1861, the Civil War began. By July 1864, Northern general William Sherman set his sights on Atlanta. As part of the siege, Sherman established his first headquarters just east of Druid Hills. Sherman's second headquarters were near the intersection of North Decatur and Briarcliff Roads. General Sherman rode on horseback through what is now Emory Village.

After the Civil War, owners of two farms returned to their homesteads. One was the Paden family, who farmed the area where the Druid Hills Golf Course is now, and the other was the Johnson family, whose farm was on today's Oakdale Road. In 1890, Johnson's heirs sold all but 10 acres of their farm to the Kirkwood Land Company.

After the war, Atlanta was a boomtown. Having been burned by General Sherman, Atlanta began to rebuild and capitalize on its location as the terminus of several railroads—Atlanta's original name being Terminus. Farms were disappearing as Atlanta expanded. Entrepreneur Joel Hurt capitalized on this growth by developing Atlanta's first suburb: Inman Park. Hurt shrewdly located his subdivision on his own street trolley so that residents could travel from the city to their homes and back, and his company would get the fare.

When Inman Park was finished, Hurt purchased more land and called this business the Kirkwood Land Company. Hurt hired Frederick Law Olmsted Sr. (1822–1903) and his firm to lay out the subdivision and create a linear park that would be the center of the new subdivision. Ponce de Leon Avenue was the main thoroughfare, which would be extended to run through the heart of Hurt's new suburb. The road was named after the famous spring that Spanish explorer Ponce de Leon supposedly searched for in America. In Atlanta, Dr. Henry Wilson claimed a spring east of Atlanta was the real "fountain of youth." Wilson named the site Ponce de Leon Springs. Atlantans flocked there by horse and carriage to partake of the healing waters. Later, a streetcar was run to the springs. So, it was natural to extend both Ponce de Leon Avenue and the streetcar line into Joel Hurt's new development.

Soon, young men from rural Georgia began to move to Atlanta to seek their fortunes. Two such men, who lived nearly identical life spans, and who were to have a major influence on Atlanta and Druid Hills, were Joel Hurt and Asa Candler. Hurt had hired Olmsted, Sr. and his firm to design the "ideal residential suburb" for Kirkwood Land Company. But developing the subdivision was expensive, and Hurt decided to sell. Fortunately, Asa Candler, who bought the company, retained Olmsted's plans.

Olmsted was working in Asheville, North Carolina, at Biltmore Estate when Hurt asked him to devise a master plan for the Kirkwood Land. Olmsted, considered the father of landscape architecture in the United States, was a brilliant choice to design Hurt's second residential development—as yet unnamed. In 1893, Olmsted provided preliminary plans for the land. The extension of Ponce de Leon Avenue (which Olmsted called "Parkway") would be constructed past the northern edge of the park, and a new streetcar line would be located within the northern edge of the park. Olmsted named lakes, parks, and subdivisions after natural features. The first and westernmost park was at the entrance to the new subdivision and was called Springdale due to Silver Bell Spring. Olmsted made an exception in naming the next park to the east: Virgilee was named in memory of a child of Joel Hurt, who had died. The next park segments were Oak Grove, named after a cluster of trees; Shady Side, due to its forest canopy; Dellwood, for its bowl-shaped indentation; and the 22-acre Deepdene, for its steeply sloping sides down to an interior creek. The first five park segments are considered pastoral, and the sixth is considered woodland. Olmsted declared that the linear park was "to be perpetually reserved for park purposes for the common use and enjoyment of the owners [of the lots of the subdivision.]"

Surrounding the linear park, Olmsted planned streets on which estate lots could be located in hopes of luring rich citizens to build homes there. The new streets just off the linear park were Springdale, Oakdale, Lullwater, and Fairview. Clifton Road already existed but was extended across the linear park to the north.

In addition to laying out the new suburb, Olmsted provided planting schemes that used both native plants and rare or exotic trees and shrubs. Joel Hurt had reserved an area for storage and care of the plants before they could be put in the ground at their final site. Olmsted renamed Peavine Creek as Lullwater Creek, as it progressed through the new subdivision, because he thought Lullwater sounded more dignified. South and north of the development, the creek retains the name of Peavine.

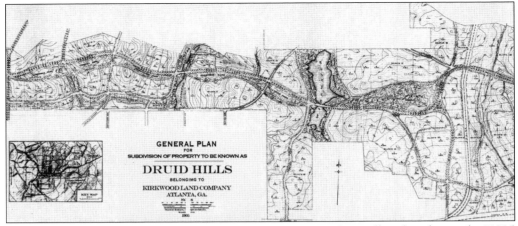

GENERAL PLAN
FOR
SUBDIVISION OF PROPERTY TO BE KNOWN AS
DRUID HILLS
BELONGING TO
KIRKWOOD LAND COMPANY
ATLANTA, GA.

DRUID HILLS

This Will Be the Name of One of Atlanta's New Suburbs.

"Druid Hills" is the name which has been given to the beautiful residential district which has been developed on Ponce de Leon parkway, under the auspices of the Kirkwood Land Company.

Information was received this week from Messrs. Olmstead Bros., landscape artists, that they had given the property this name. So the community will be known hereafter as "Druid Hills."

The name is both significant and appropriate. The district consists of a succession of broad plateaus, which have been clothed by nature with the sturdy oak, and which the word "Druid" signifies.

About 100 acres of the property, which has been undergoing improvements for several years,, is now to be offered for sale for the first time. The lots are large, varying size from an acre and a half to five acres. They have been improved, drained and planted in blue grass and shrubbery in an elaborate style. This planting is now over two years old, and is beginning to show the artist's design. It only remains for the buildings to be placed in position, when the entire landscape will appear in harmony.

Generally referred to as the "1905 map," this shows Frederick Law Olmsted's design for Ponce de Leon Parkway, the Linear Park, and portions of some of the side streets that intersected Ponce de Leon. Note that the map shows Lullwater and Widewater Lakes, which were never constructed. The site for the clubhouse became the estate of Lucy Candler Heinz, and the golf club was located at the corner of Clifton Road and Ponce de Leon Avenue. (Courtesy of OLPA and the National Park Service, Frederick Law Olmsted National Historic Site.)

An April 30, 1905, newspaper article announces that Druid Hills has been given a name. Joel Hurt asked for possible names, and Olmsted replied with 37 suggestions, including Lochrest, Vernonchase, Etowah, Hills of Arden, New Dorp, Merrymount, Bonnybrae, and Druidhills (note that Olmsted's suggestion was one word). Hurt chose Druidhills and separated it into two words, capitalizing the "H" in Hills. Thus, Druid Hills was born. (Courtesy of the *Atlanta Journal-Constitution*.)

One

DRUID HILLS IS BORN

Joel Hurt (1850–1926) formed the Kirkwood Land Company and asked Olmsted for some name suggestions for his project. On September 15, 1904, Olmsted responded with a list of 37 proposed names.

In 1886, Asa Griggs Candler (1851–1929) purchased the formula for a "brain tonic" for $2,300 that had been developed by pharmacist John Pemberton. who called this concoction "French Wine Cola Nerve Tonic." Its syrup was mixed with carbonated water and first sold in 1886 at Jacob's drugstore in downtown Atlanta under the name Coca-Cola. What made Coca-Cola stand out from hundreds of competing tonics was Candler's brilliant advertising and his decision to allow the drink to be bottled. The ability to purchase it in bottles meant one could purchase Coca-Cola to serve at home. Coca-Cola made Asa Candler rich and famous. Candler went on to serve as the 41st mayor of Atlanta and become the city's wealthiest citizen.

The lives and fortunes of Joel Hurt and Asa Candler converged on the real estate transaction Hurt had made to buy land for his second suburb. In 1908, Hurt sold his Kirkwood Land Company to four prominent Atlantans for $500,000—the largest real estate deal in Atlanta to that date. The new owners were Asa Candler, Preston Arkwright (1871–1946), and brothers Forrest (1863–1936), and George Adair (1873–1921.) The four new owners retained the services of Frederick Law Olmsted Sr. and his firm.

Asa Candler was the president of the Druid Hills Corporation. Because of his great wealth, he could afford to be a generous benefactor. He donated land in 1916 to build an Atlanta campus of the Oxford College of Emory University in Oxford, Georgia. He donated money to help build what would become Emory University, Wesley Memorial Hospital, and the Candler School of Theology at Emory. Because of his prominence and wealth, Candler and all of his children built palatial residences in Druid Hills. One cannot imagine Druid Hills without the Candler family and all their exploits.

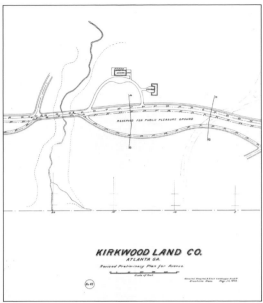

This 1893 clipping shows where Olmsted planned a public clubhouse and Casino. In those days, a casino was not for gambling, but an outdoor pavilion where picnics, concerts, and dances could be held. (Courtesy of Sue Sullivan)

Frederick Law Olmsted's son Frederick Jr. and his stepson John Charles came to Atlanta in 1902 to photograph the Druid Hills land for their father. Olmsted Sr. could then use the images to perfect his landscape designs. The land was over farmed, filled with Jack Pines, and had been the scene of some skirmishes during the Civil War. It was ugly and unkempt. The dark ditch on the bottom left of the photograph is Lullwater Creek. From center left into the distance is the current site of Shady Side Park. (Courtesy of the National Park Service, Frederick Law Olmsted National Historic Site.)

This photograph is another of the series taken by the two Olmsted brothers. The original conditions of this land were decrepit, yet Olmsted Sr. was able to transform the land into today's Linear Park. (Courtesy of the National Park Service, Frederick Law Olmsted National Historic Site.)

Headlines in The Atlanta Journal on May 19, 1908, heralded the historic sale of Joel Hurt's Kirkwood Land Company to Asa Candler for half a million dollars. Brothers Forrest and George Adair, pictured beneath the banner, had been associated with Candler ever since the turn of the century when Candler became wealthy from Coca-Cola. The Adairs were instrumental in the purchase of most of Candler's extensive holdings, including the present Hartsfield International Airport site.

Joel Hurt was a visionary who developed a street railroad system and Atlanta's Inman Park and owned the Kirkwood Land Company. He is credited with hiring Olmsted Sr. and naming the subdivision Druid Hills. (Courtesy of Dr. James Bryant and Druid Hills Golf Course.)

...agents in charge of all property hold-

...the same time, Asa Candler conveyed ...incorporators of Druid Hills the newly-...hased tract of land from Kirkwood Land ...pany comprising 1,492 wooded acres in ...t had been heralded by the Atlanta Jour-...n May 19, 1908, the largest real estate ...saction ever made in the South.[3] Nego-...ns for the purchase had been under way ...everal months, with George Adair han-...g the transaction from beginning to end.

JOEL HURT AND THE OLMSTEDS

...el Hurt, a civil and landscaping engineer ...ofession and voluntary student of hor-...ture, had assembled the vast wooded ...hilly acreage for a residential commu-...on the northeastern edge of Atlanta, ...el after parcel and farm after farm.[4] Hurt ...t the assembled property as a single en-

Company, a corporation organized and managed by himself, until 1908. At the time of the sale the property had been surveyed and the principal streets outlined, but there was no paving.[5] A land map drawn in 1905 by the Olmsted Brothers of Massachusetts shows land lot divisions, parks, and major arteries, together with the golf course and a proposed site for the clubhouse.

At least eighteen years prior to the sale, Joel Hurt had planned the entire property as a suburban residential park. In April 1892 he bought the last property parcel needed for his garden residential community and a month later hired landscape architect Frederick Law Olmsted to design an "ideal residential suburb." Olmsted (best known for designing New York's Central Park (1858), the U. S. Capitol grounds (1874), and the Biltmore Estate grounds (1888) in Asheville, North Carolina) was reluctant. By then he was seventy-one years old, in failing health, and hesitant to travel long distances. But

a plan for Druid Hills that included gently curving avenues and naturalistic landscaping, characteristics of Olmsted's trademark style.

Olmsted made a preliminary survey of the forests, drew the stretch of Ponce de Leon Avenue (he called it a "parkway") that forms the backbone of the neighborhood, designed the chain of linear parks and the main roads through Druid Hills (Oakdale, Springdale, and Lullwater) and delivered his original plan to Hurt in 1893.[6]

Although Olmsted came to Atlanta in March 1894 to consult on what later became Piedmont Park, he had to retire in 1895 before the master plan could be implemented. Actually, in 1893 an economic depression struck the nation, resulting six years later in possible bankruptcy for the Kirkwood Land Company while Joel Hurt was engaging in a dispute with H. M. Atkinson over their respective power, light, and streetcar interests, and after several loans had been made

13

In 1909, a stockholder letter outlined the improvements the Druid Hills Corporation had made to the property after purchasing it. (Courtesy of Rose Library at Emory University.)

2/7/1909

TO THE STOCKHOLDERS
OF DRUID HILLS.

Gentlemen:

We beg to report that the improvements on Ponce de Leon Avenue North and Ponce de Leon Avenue South, from Moreland Avenue to Lullwater Road, including water, gas, sewerage and macadam, have been completed, leaving only the cement sidewalk yet to be laid.

We would also report that after considerable delay, the concrete bridge has been finished, and, while the cost is more than we first anticipated, we believe we have a splendid structure.

The water and gas mains have already been laid on the Fairview Road; the sewer is now being put down and the contract for macadam pavement has been let, the work to begin as soon as the sewer work has been finished.

Contractors are now at work grading the Oakdale and Springdale Roads and Ponce de Leon Avenue North to the Decatur Road; a distance of about 6300 feet for Springdale Road, and 6600 feet for Oakdale Road.

It is our intention, as soon as the grading has been completed, to put down, sewer, water, gas, macadam pavement and tiled sidewalk on these two streets, so as to have them ready for the market.

As soon as the grading on these two Roads have been completed, we recommend that Ponce de Leon Avenue North and Ponce de Leon Avenue South be brought to a proper grade from the Lullwater Bridge east to a point on the Georgia Railroad that will meet the new Boulevard that has been graded from that point to East Lake; and, that after water, sewer and gas mains have been laid, Ponce de Leon Avenue be paved with macadam for it's entire length.

From the work we have actually done at Druid Hills and from the estimates made by our Engineer, Mr. Kauffman, we have ascertained that the cost per front foot to each lot for these improvements is as follows:

Water,   35 cents,
Gas,   32 cents
Sewer,   25 cents
Paving,   95 cents
Sidewalk,   27 cents,   making a total of $2.14 per lineal foot.

Asa Candler donated land and a million dollars to bring Emory College to Atlanta in 1916. It was rechartered as Emory University. Henry Hornbostle was hired to design the buildings, but in fact, Louis Edmund Crook and Ed Ivey did most of the work.

117—Aerial View, Emory University, Atlanta, Ga.

Two

THE FIRST FAMILY OF DRUID HILLS

After arriving in Atlanta, Asa Candler first worked as a pharmacist and clerk in a drugstore in downtown Atlanta owned by George Howard. It was in Howard's drugstore that Candler met Howard's young daughter, Lucy Elizabeth Howard. In 1878, the couple married. The Candlers had five children. Charles Howard was born in 1878, followed by Asa Griggs Candler Jr., who was called "Buddie," born in 1880. Lucy Beall Candler was born in 1883, Walter Turner in 1885, and William in 1890. As the family grew, they moved to bigger and better homes. This was especially true after 1886, when Asa Candler purchased the Coca-Cola formula and began amassing his fortune. In 1901, Buddie married Helen McGill. Lucy Junior married William Owens in 1903. Charles Howard married Flora Glenn in 1903. In 1907, Walter Candler married Eugenia Bingham, and in 1913, William married Bennie Teabeaut. In 1914, Asa's son-in-law Bill Owens, who had married Lucy Jr. died. In 1916, Asa Candler gave 75 acres and a huge donation to establish Emory University in Atlanta. Also in 1916, Asa and Lucy moved into their third and most opulent home, called the Lemon Pie House.

Asa and Lucy Candler's first home in Druid Hills was on Ponce de Leon Avenue. The family called it the "Lemon Pie House" because its construction was of yellow bricks and white marble. On December 25, 1917, Asa handed each of his children an envelope containing their inheritance: the Coca-Cola Company. After the death of Lucy Sr. in 1919, Asa remained at this home and began giving the last of his fortune away. His five children sold the company to Ernest Woodruff, Asa's bitter enemy. When he learned his children had sold his company, he was furious. Later in life, Asa was plagued by a well-publicized romance. He met a socialite from New Orleans named Onezima de Bouchel Roquet, fell in love with her, and wanted to marry her, but Madame Roquet was mainly interested in Candler's money—not knowing he had given it away. Asa's children broke up the marriage plans. Madame Roquet sued Asa for breach of promise, and during the trial, which Asa won, his love letters to her were printed in the Atlanta papers.

Callanwolde was the Tudor Revival home of Charles Howard Candler and his wife, Flora Glenn Candler, designed by Henry Hornbostle, who also designed some of the buildings at Emory University. The Candlers and their three children moved into the 24-room mansion in 1920. On the 27-acre property, Callanwolde had a pool, servants' quarters, greenhouses, and gardens. Flora endowed the Glenn Memorial Methodist Church and the Flora Glenn Candler Concert Series at Emory. An accomplished musician, Flora often played the piano or the Aeolian pipe organ in the great hall. When Flora was not playing, she could insert organ rolls into the organ, and it would play itself. Charles died in 1957, and the estate was sold to Emory, who sold to the First Christian Church. The house fell into decline and was rescued from the wrecking ball by the DeKalb Council for the Arts and the DeKalb Federation of Garden Clubs (and others). Today, Callanwolde is an arts and cultural center.

Buddie Candler owned 42 acres on Briarcliff Road, which had a modest house and farm. As his family grew, he commissioned a colossal Georgian Revival mansion designed by Charles E. Frazier and Dan Bodin in 1920. In 1925, the home was enlarged, adding a massive music room with Aeolian organ. The estate included sweeping terraces, greenhouses, servants' quarters, garages, a laundry, nine-hole golf course, swimming pools, and stables. (Courtesy of Sue Sullivan.)

This close-up of Buddie Candler's Briarcliff Botanical Gardens shows swimmers in waist-high water. The building with columns and arches is the pool pavilion. Entrance to the pool was 25¢. Coca-Cola and snacks were sold on the main floor. Dressing rooms were in the basement. The large object at center left was the fountain, which was illuminated with colored lights at night. (Courtesy of Julia Wynne.)

This photograph shows an aerial view of Briarcliff Estate after its sale to the State of Georgia. The mansion, top left, became the Georgian Clinic—the first treatment center for alcoholism in the state. The tower and cottages were part of Georgia Mental Health Institute and were built where the farm, dairy, and laundry once stood.

Buddie Candler was in Europe when he bought a circus and wired home the following: "Bought circus, build zoo." Cages were made ready on the estate. The zoo animals arrived by train at the depot at Emory University, Georgia, and handlers escorted them on foot up to Briarcliff. Many Druid Hills residents turned out to watch the parade of exotic animals, such as giraffes and lions, walk past. This image appeared in an April 1932 article. (Courtesy of the *Atlanta Journal-Constitution*.)

Lucy Candler married William Owens Sr. in 1903. The couple, who had two children, lived in a house on Little Ponce de Leon. The house was later known as "Mother Goose" because of a nursery that later occupied the building. Lucy and her husband developed typhoid, and William Sr. died. Lucy was too ill to attend his funeral. Lucy and her children moved into the Lemon Pie house.

Lucy Candler married banker Henry Heinz in 1917. The couple hired architect Lloyd Preacher to design their magnificent Mediterranean estate on Ponce de Leon Avenue. The Heinz mansion was named Rainbow Terrace. No expense was spared in the construction of the house. The mansion sat on a rise with a lawn dotted with flowering dogwoods sweeping to Ponce de Leon Avenue. Many of the rooms had hand-carved beams and medallions, with plaster walls washed in pale hues. (Courtesy of DeKalb History Center.)

The opulence of Rainbow Terrace was an elegant backdrop for parties, family dinners, and social occasions. Henry and Lucy Heinz raised two children there: Mimi and Henry Heinz Jr. Lucy Heinz's daughter Elizabeth Owens had her formal debut there, followed by dinner at the Druid Hills Golf Club, and she was later married at the home. After her honeymoon, she and her husband, Dr. Vann, moved into Rainbow Terrace. (Courtesy of DeKalb History Center.)

In 1943, tragedy struck the Heinz family. An intruder entered Rainbow Terrace in a robbery attempt. Henry Heinz, who was in his library, struggled with the assailant and was shot four times and died almost instantly. Lucy left the house that evening and never lived there again, instead going to an apartment at the Biltmore Hotel. Lucy eventually moved to New York and married former Atlanta Symphony conductor Enrico Leide. (Courtesy of DeKalb History Center.)

Walter Candler's first home faced North Decatur Road but had a Lullwater Road address. Behind the home, he built stables, a harness racing track, and housing for farmworkers. He also built a log cabin for recreational purposes, facing Emory Road, which he sold in 1929. He sold portions of his amassed 34-acre property for lots that became the "College Streets" section of Druid Hills. (Courtesy of Sue Sullivan.)

This is Walter Candler's first log cabin or clubhouse. It is still standing today and is a private residence. Candler decorated it with rustic furniture and hung stuffed animal heads from his hunting trips on the walls. (Courtesy of Sue Sullivan.)

Walter Candler was the fourth child and third son of Lucy and Asa Candler. After moving from his first home, He built his Tudor Revival mansion on a huge tract of land, calling it Lullwater Farms. The house was designed by Ivey and Crook, using timber and rocks from the estate. (Courtesy of Sue Sullivan)

This article appeared in the *Atlanta Constitution* in 1923 and detailed the opening of Walter Candler's new racetrack. Barbeque was served before the race to about 500 guests. The best horses in the south came to compete. Candler met 21-year-old Sarah Byfield at a race event, and despite Sarah being married, they became close friends. (See more on page 25.) (Courtesy of the *Atlanta Journal-Constitution*.)

Walter Candler purchased a large tract of land between Clifton and Clairmont Roads, which he dubbed Lullwater Farms. He commissioned Ivey and Crook to construct a Tudor Revival mansion on a hilltop using building materials from the property. The estate had two barns, two harness race tracks, a clubhouse (pictured), grandstand, electric power plant, farm, and lake. (Courtesy of Rose Library at Emory University.)

Sarah Byfield (left) and Marion Candler (right) stand in front of a scoreboard at the race track. In 1922, Walter Candler invited Sarah and Clyde Byfield to go on a cruise, leaving Mrs. Candler behind. Sarah alleged Walter entered her room, tore the bedclothes, and "disheveled" her nightgown. When Clyde arrived, a fight ensued between the men. The Byfields sued Walter for $100,000 for assault and lost. Walter claimed they were trying to extort money from him. (Courtesy of Sue Sullivan.)

In 1913, Bennie Teabeaut and William Candler married and built Rest Haven on Springdale Road, designed by Neel Reid. The couple had two children: Rena and William. Built in 1915, the home sat on 21 acres with a pond, stables, and gardens. The original plot of land extended all the way to the By Way. Candler sold off parts of his property, as he needed the money.

TO GEORGE SPENCE

Mishap Occurs Close to Naylor as Pair Are on Way Westward From Waycross: Details of Tragedy Not Learned.

CAR IS OVERTURNED BY SHARP IMPACT

Victim Was Elected Head of Biltmore Corporation in 1930 and Was Manager of Hotel.

William Candler, 46, son of the late Asa Candler and prominent Atlanta hotel man and civic leader, was instantly killed at about 11 o'clock last night when the automobile he was driving struck a cow and overturned on Highway 38,

WILLIAM CANDLER.

In 1936, William Candler was killed in an automobile crash while en route back to Atlanta from his investment land in Florida. He was 46. A cow wandered onto the highway and was struck by William's car, which overturned. Rest Haven was sold after his death by his widow and today is a private residence. (Courtesy of the *Atlanta Journal-Constitution*.)

The Judge John S. Candler home was the first built in Druid Hills in 1909 and the first demolished (in 1957). This 1925 picture shows the Candler home, designed by G.L. Norman, at the corner of Briarcliff Road and Ponce de Leon at the entrance to Druid Hills. In 1957, the Druid Hills Methodist Church, designed by Ivey and Crook was built on the lot. (Courtesy of Helen McSwain.)

Judge Candler is pictured here with two of his grandchildren. He had a total of eight grandchildren. Asa Warren's children were John II, Asa Warren Jr., Robert, William, and a daughter named Mardivi. Daughter Florrie Guy had three children: Candler, Samuel James, and Allie Guy. (Courtesy of Helen McSwain.)

This photograph shows Allie Candler and two friends framing their faces with tennis rackets on the backyard tennis court of Judge John Candler. The judge's family was enthusiastic tennis players and often arose at 6:00 a.m. to play the game. (Courtesy of Helen McSwain.)

Judge John S. Candler is pictured standing on the porch of his home with daughter Allie Candler, who is holding a bouquet of flowers. The judge and his daughter were en route to Allie's graduation from Agnes Scott College in Decatur, Georgia. (Courtesy of Helen McSwain.)

The Georgian Revival home of Asa Warren Candler Jr. is shown in the 1930s. The home was designed by Neel Reid. Apparently, the home was never given a name. After the death of the family, the home was sold to the Catholic Church. The Monastery of the Visitation was installed in the house. The nuns were cloistered. Their occupation was to bake communion bread for Catholic churches, and they passed the bread to purchasers through a hole in a high wooden fence, which still exists. (Courtesy of Helen McSwain.)

Each of the Candler homes had elaborate landscaped gardens, pools, and fountains. This picture shows the garden behind the Asa Warren Candler Jr. home. A gardener employed by the family is standing at the left rear. (Courtesy of Helen McSwain.)

This Georgian Revival home, designed by Ivey and Crook, was built in 1929 for the John H. Candler family. It is located on Lullwater Road. It has been completely renovated with additions and improvements to the house and garden and remains a private home today.

This home on Lullwater Parkway was given as a wedding present by Charles Howard Candler Sr. to his son Charles Howard Candler Jr. and his wife, Ruth, in 1929. The couple had four children. Today, the house still exists as a private home with its original footprint from Philip Shutze's plans and is a meticulous example of historic preservation. (Courtesy of Charles Candler Lovett and Gail and Spencer King.)

Four Candler children are shown leaning against Charles Howard Candler Jr.'s car. To the left of the garage, there's a flat area past the woods, where one of Buddie Candler's zoo elephants is said to be buried. The floor above the garage was called the "Trophy Room" and contained many examples of taxidermy. This is one of many of the Candler "cabins" used to display hunting trophies. (Courtesy of Charles Candler Lovett and Gail and Spencer King.)

Three

RICH AND INFLUENTIAL CITIZENS BUILD IN DRUID HILLS

As soon as it was known that the Candlers were involved in Druid Hills, other wealthy families decided to purchase lots and build their homes there as well. Amongst the new buyers were the DeGives, Dodsons, Stones, Pattillos, Woolfords, Kings, Venables, Rainwaters, Arkwrights, Adairs, and others. Jewish families also flocked to Druid Hills. Unlike many housing developments in Atlanta, Asa Candler put no restrictions whatsoever on Jews living in Druid Hills. Jews felt welcomed, and a great many became residents including the Lowenstein, Rich, Strauss, Regenstein, Montag, and Elsas families. Many families had one of Atlanta's famous architects design their home. The premier architects of the day were Edward E. Dougherty (1876–1943), J. Neel Reid (1885–1926), Philip Shutze (1890–1982), Arthur Neal Robinson (1886–1958), Robert Smith Pringle (1883–1937), Edmund Louis Crook (1898–1967), Francis Palmer Smith 1886–1971), DeFord Smith (1894–1952), Charles Frazier (1883–1939), Walter T. Downing 1865–1918) Ed Ivey (1887–1966), Owen Southwell (1892–1961), Leila Ross Wilburn (1885–1967), Henry Hornbostle (1867–1961), Geoffrey Lloyd Preacher (1882–1972), Dan Bodin (1895–1963), and A. Ten Eyck Brown (1878–1940) Noted landscape architect Thomas Cridland (1890–1930) designed two gardens in Druid Hills, that of Cator Woolford (around the 1920s) and the Harris Garden (1921) on South Ponce de Leon. Popular housing styles for the citizens of Druid Hills included Georgian, Colonial, Tudor, Italian Renaissance, and Spanish revival. Other designs include the Four Square, Craftsman, Bungalow, and English Manor. The large lots, gracious houses, and tree-lined streets made Druid Hills a desirable place in which to buy a home.

Pinebloom was the Tudor Revival mansion of Preston and Dorothy Arkwright. Preston was the president of the Georgia Power Company and Atlanta Street Railway Company, and Dorothy was the daughter of the governor of Georgia. The home, designed by Walter T. Downing (1865–1918), was built in 1914 and had 18 rooms and a ballroom on the third floor. The gardens of Pinebloom were featured in *Garden History of Georgia, 1733–1933*.

After Preston Arkwright's death in 1947, the home and 12 surrounding acres were sold to the Georgia Baptist Broadcasting group, who used the third-floor ballroom for radio production. Later, it was purchased by the Jackson Hill Baptist Church, who built a sanctuary adjacent to the church in 1957. This is a photograph of the rear elevation of Pinebloom.

Preston Arkwright and Joel Hurt both supported public transportation and owned streetcar companies. This photograph shows trolley No. 618 going through Druid Hills on tracks within Olmsted's Oak Grove Park. Main Ponce de Leon is on the left, South Ponce de Leon is to the far right, and the Druid Hills Garden Club memorial granite fountain is in the middle of the park. (Courtesy of the Atlanta History Center.)

Jacqueland was the Ponce de Leon estate of Retail Credit Company founder Cator Woolford. The house was designed by Owen Southwell in a Georgian Revival style and sat high atop a hill overlooking gardens designed by Thomas Cridland. The estate contained greenhouses, ponds, tennis courts, a nine-hole golf course, woodland, trails, and streams. Woolford married the former Charlotte Boyd and had two children: Isabel and Charlotte Jr. (Courtesy of Cator Sparks, great-grandson of Cator Woolford.)

A birthday party for one of the Woolford girls is held on the lawn of Jacqueland, with the tennis house in the background, Cator Woolford stands at far-right front. The tables are laden with food and flowers. Today, these gardens are used for weddings and events. (Courtesy of Cator Sparks, great-grandson of Cator Woolford.)

Isabel (left) and Charlotte Jr. (right) Woolford led privileged lives. They had their own house large enough for a whole family, with tea sets and sterling silver, and they rode around the Jacqueland estate on electric cars, such as the one in the picture. (Courtesy of Cator Sparks, great-grandson of Cator Woolford.)

A collage of Druid Hills scenes was used to advertise the desirability of the area. Brothers Forrest and George Adair were investors in the Druid Hills Corporation, and the exclusive realtors used to market the lots and homes. The Villa is pictured top right in the collage and was the home of George Adair. At top left is a view of the bridge crossing Lullwater Creek. The other scenes are unidentified. The photograph below is a 1920s postcard showing Ponce de Leon. In the foreground is the Clyde L. King Home, the Jackson family home is in the middle, and the home of Forrest Adair is in the background. Both Adairs and their families enjoyed the game of golf and helped to found the Druid Hills Golf Course (in 1912).

Druid Hills,   ATLANTA, Ga.

This postcard shows the home of George Adair, which he called the Villa. The Walter Browne Company did all the interior decorating. Behind the home, Adair built a huge swimming pool and pavilion designed by Neel Reid. Both the pool and the home have been demolished—the home was replaced by Lion's Gate Condominiums. In the 1930s and 1940s, huge homes such as this one were being turned into boardinghouses.

Stonehenge was the home of Hoyt Venable and his family. It was designed by Edward Emmet Dougherty (1876–1943) and built in 1914. Venable owned Stone Mountain, east of Atlanta, which is the largest granite outcropping in the United States. The giant granite blocks used for Stonehenge were quarried from Stone Mountain. The structure is considered English domestic Gothic style. (Courtesy of Sue Sullivan.)

Hoyt Venable was a bachelor and lived in the gigantic home with members of his extended family. Venable's sister was an artist who painted many beautiful murals throughout the home as seen in the next photograph. Venable was a grand dragon (leader) in the Ku Klux Klan in the 1920s and allowed the group to burn crosses on top of Stone Mountain. He was also instrumental in having Gutzon Borglum commissioned to create the Confederate Memorial carving on the side of a mountain. (Courtesy of Sue Sullivan.)

Arthur Tufts was a builder for Asa Candler and helped construct many of the buildings on Emory's campus. Tufts purchased 25 acres on Clifton Road and constructed a three-story pink stucco mansion that he called Woodland House. A drive served the home, with upper and lower gates—which led to streets named Uppergate and Lowergate. Tufts supervised construction at Emory until his death in 1920. (Courtesy of Rose Library at Emory University.)

The Tufts family poses on the terrace of Woodland House in the late 1900s. From left to right are Arthur Tufts Jr., John Tufts, Joanne Wilcox Tufts (in arms of her mother), Anna Rutledge Tufts, and Rutledge Tufts. (Courtesy of Rose Library at Emory University.)

The home of Harry J. Carr was located on Springdale Road and designed by Leila Ross Wilburn (1885–1967), one of two women architects in Atlanta in the 1920s. The Carr family moved from this home to a home Carr built called Houston Mill House, which was then out in the country on Houston Mill Road. Houston Mill House had a lake, mill, dam, horse stables, and a spring-fed swimming pool. (Courtesy of Dekalb History Center.)

This photograph is of the front of Houston Mill House, built by Harry Carr., owner of H.J. Carr Construction Company. The house consisted of 14 rooms and was made of stone found on the property. It was on a vast amount of land that had belonged to Major Houston. Carr ground corn into meal at the mill, which was located next to the south fork of Peachtree Creek.

This is a delightful shot of the front of Houston Mill House in which the Carr children are seen playing. They also enjoyed the swimming pool across Houston Mill Road and riding their horses in the woods. The children are Francis (left) and Gladys (right) Carr. Harry Carr renovated the grain mill and built the swimming pool and pool house, hydroelectric plant, and two water storage tanks. (Courtesy of Rose Library at Emory University.)

The Carr family's pool is shown in this photograph. It was fed by spring water. It had three diving boards and a pool house. Harry Carr also built trails, bridges, and a swinging bridge to have access to his extensive property. (Courtesy of Rose Library at Emory University.)

An iron bridge across the south fork of Peachtree Creek connected the east and west segments of Houston Mill Road. The metal bridge was later replaced with a concrete one, and a curve was straightened out when Houston Mill Road was improved. The metal bridge is still standing but unusable. To the right of the bridge is the millpond. (Courtesy of Rose Library at Emory University.)

El Paradisio was the name of the Fenn Stone mansion, designed by Louis Edmund Crook (1898–1967) in 1923. The Italian Renaissance Revival home sat on the highest point in Druid Hills and had greenhouses, servants' quarters, and a sunken Japanese tea garden. Italian craftsmen were commissioned to do all the interior work on the home. Fenn Stone made his fortune from his bakeries and he and his wife, Princess, raised their daughter Donna in El Paradisio. (Courtesy of Ivey and Crook.)

Glenwoods was the Tudor Revival home of "Buck" and Clara Dodson. It was designed by Walter Downing in 1918. Buck made his fortune from patent medicines made by his Ironized Yeast Company, which produced ironized yeast tablets and Dodson's Liver Tone. These products were guaranteed to fix whatever ailed you. After the death of Clara in 1968, the home was sold and remains a private home. (Courtesy of Sue Sullivan.)

Glenwoods estate included acres of gardens that had trails, a stone bridge, a boxwood maze, a gazebo, cutting gardens, ponds, streams, waterfalls, and a garden house built to resemble a stone chapel. Unfortunately, the gardens were removed in the late 1960s when the Dorchester Apartments (now Lullwater Parc Condominiums) were built. (Courtesy of Sue Sullivan.)

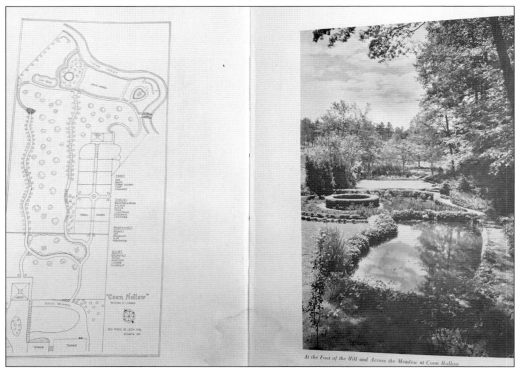

Coon Hollow was the name of Lorraine and R.L. Cooneys' property. The home sat close to Ponce de Leon Avenue but had a yard that was 800 feet deep. The Cooneys built rock steps leading down to a replica of a Scottish chapel, grotto, overlook, formal gardens mazes, and ponds. This photograph shows a plan for the garden design. Lorraine Cooney was the editor of *Garden History of Georgia, 1733–1933*. The house still stands and is owned by Fernbank. (Courtesy of Cherokee Garden Library, Atlanta History Center.)

The Oliver Willoughby home was a Tudor Revival mansion on Ponce de Leon. Oliver was a publisher of medical books. The baby in this photograph is daughter Marie Willoughby, who grew up to love gardening and plants and become a lifelong member of the Georgia Appalachian Trail Club. She was close friends of Emily Harrison of Fernbank and Lorraine Cooney, who edited *Garden History of Georgia, 1733–1933.*

In 1968, the Willoughby family sold their home to Fernbank, Inc. and moved to a ranch house on nearby Clifton Terrace. Fernbank, Inc. was acquiring property along Ponce de Leon in order to construct its Museum of Natural History. Of the seven homes Fernbank purchased, three were demolished, including Twin Oaks and the Willoughby house.

One of playwright Alfred Uhry's relatives lived in this home on Ponce de Leon, and another, Lena Fox, his grandmother, lived on Fairview Road. The writer based his character Miss Daisy in *Driving Miss Daisy* on the two women. The playwright, who attended Druid Hills High School, was honored by having the theater/auditorium named for him. The play was very popular and made into a movie that was filmed in Druid Hills.

The Boxwood is located on Springdale Road. It was the home of the Veazey Rainwater family. Veazy Rainwater was responsible for the design of the Coke bottle. The estate originally included a two-story boys' clubhouse, paddock, barn, pond, grandstand, cutting garden, and wild garden. Rainwater made his fortune with the Coca-Cola Company.

The Clyde King home was on Ponce de Leon. Clyde Lanier King owned King Plow Company. One of King's daughters, Irene, married George Woodruff, brother of Robert. The gardens of the King home were opened to the public each year. Clyde's wife, Clara Bell King, wished to be buried in the garden, but that was not allowed. A replica of the home became a monument to her at Oakland Cemetery. Today, the home is the headquarters of Alpha Delta Pi women's sorority.

Robert Ison (left) and Dave Ison (right) had their own goat and goat cart. Here, they are posing in front of 1793 South Ponce de Leon Avenue, which was the home of their paternal grandparents, Roswell Davis Ison and Hilda Watson Ison. (Courtesy of Lindsey Sones.)

The Frank E. Lowenstein home was designed by Pringle and Smith during 1919–1922 for one of two Lowenstein brothers (Max was the other), who owned the Norris Candy Company, which made chocolate and fruit candy. Max's home, also designed by Pringle and Smith, was later purchased by Paideia School. The Frank E. Lowenstein home eventually became a Unity church and, later, home to the Atlanta Boy Choir.

This splendid home on Oakdale Road belonged to the Sigmund Montag family. It was designed by architect Neel Reid in 1915. The Montags owned a paper company and made, among other things, the famous Blue Horse tablets for schoolchildren. The scene in the film *Driving Miss Daisy* in which Daisy drives off the driveway actually occurred at this house and was filmed here.

The Louis Jacob Elsas home, located on Oakdale Road, was designed by Neel Reid and built in 1913. Elsas was vice president of the Fulton Bag and Cotton Mill located in Cabbagetown, south of Druid Hills. One of the characters in Alfred Uhry's play *Driving Miss Daisy* (Boolie) is probably based upon Elsas.

The Walter Rich house, designed by Neel Reid, is located on Fairview Road. It was constructed in the French manor style and built in 1913. Walter was son of one of the three brothers who founded Rich's Department Store. He was president of Rich's from 1926 to 1947.

This Italian-style home was designed in 1917 by Neel Reid for the Louis Regenstein family. The family owned a women's clothing shop (called Regenstein's) that sold fashionable and expensive clothing to Atlanta's wealthy women. The flagship store was in downtown Atlanta on Peachtree Street. The family sold the business in the 1970s.

The modest one-story Guy home still stands at the corner of Oxford Road and North Decatur Road. Allie Candler, the daughter of Judge John Candler, attended Agnes Scott College and then married Samuel Guy, professor of chemistry at Emory. The couple raised their four children there. This house still remains in the Candler family. (Courtesy of Helen McSwain.)

Allie Candler married Samuel Guy at the home of Judge Candler. The photograph shows the entire wedding party posing in the dining room of the home. Many of the furnishings remain in the Candler family today. (Courtesy of Helen McSwain.)

Robert Woodruff and his wife, Nell Hodgson Woodruff, purchased this home on Springdale Road, which was designed by Neel Reid in 1919. The Woodruffs lived in the home from 1919 until 1948, when they relocated to Buckhead. Robert was the son of Ernest Woodruff, purchaser of the Coca-Cola Company. Nell was the sister of Dr. Grady Hodgson, who built Wildwoods in the Fernbank Forest. (Courtesy of Rose Library at Emory University.)

The hunting lodge of Robert Woodruff was located on what is now Briardale Lane, but the property was originally part of Woodruff's large estate on Springdale Road. The rustic lodge was made of logs and contained cabin-type furniture and stuffed animal trophies on the walls. This lodge still stands and is a private home. (Courtesy of Rose Library at Emory University.)

This home was designed by Neel Reid for himself and his mother. It is located on Fairview Road and remains a private home.

Robert Smith Pringle was another of Druid Hill's popular architects. He designed and built his white clapboard home on Lullwater Road. For years, this house remained in decay. New owners have restored the house to perfection. During their renovation, they found many of Pringle's architectural drawings of Georgia Institute of Technology, which they donated to the school. (Courtesy of Sue Sullivan.)

Architect Walter T. Downing designed and built his Tudor Revival Home on Oakdale Road. This home is one of the few that shares a circular drive with the house next door.

In the backyard of the Walter T. Downing home, a day nursery and kindergarten was operated by a young Antoinette Johnson Matthews, who would later run her own out-of-doors school on Oakdale Road. This was long before public schools offered this service. (Courtesy of the Georgia Archives.)

Dr. Grady Lake lived in this Ivey and Crook designed home on Ponce de Leon Avenue. It was constructed in 1926 and is the only one of the homes along that stretch of Ponce de Leon that Fernbank, Inc., did not buy. Dr. Lake was one of—if not the first—chiropractor in Atlanta.

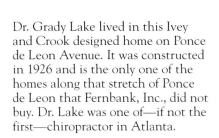

Geoffrey Lloyd Preacher designed and constructed this Mediterranean Revival home on South Ponce de Leon for himself and his family. His trademark was to build a child's playhouse in the backyards of his designs. Preacher designed Rainbow Terrace, but the playhouse at that site has been demolished. At the Preacher home, the child's playhouse still stands. The house is now a private residence, and the owners have thoroughly and lovingly restored the home.

Home of Mr. and Mrs. Robert Anderson Sewell, Ponce de Leon Avenue, Atlanta.

George Willis built this home at the corner of Clifton Road and Ponce de Leon and called it Twin Oaks. Willis made a fortune selling patent medicines. He used some of that money to purchase Engleside, a small community and farmland east of Druid Hills. There, Willis developed Avondale Estates, Georgia—a planned community with a Tudor Revival shopping area, lake and other amenities. The Tudor shops were designed by Arthur Neal Robinson, and the landscaping was done by Robert Cridland. This house no longer stands.

This "mystery house" stood at the corner of East Lake Road and Ponce de Leon Avenue. Little is currently known about it, including architect, date of construction or who lived there. It was demolished when the Saint Elias Antiochian Orthodox Church built their sanctuary on the site. (Courtesy Saint Elias Antiochian Orthodox Church.)

Dr. Grady Hodgson purchased land from Col. Zadock Harrison in Fernbank Forest. The house was named "Wildwoods." Dr. Hodgson served in the Emory Corps in World War I, and his sister married Robert Woodruff.

Four

EXPANSION IN
THE 1920S–1960S

As the population of Atlanta increased, additional streets were laid out and houses built. One of the first was Druid Hills Heights, villa architecture by James Turner and landscape design by Henry Jordan, built in 1925. The Mediterranean Revival homes sat high atop a hill, and each home had a lush garden. A section of Druid Hills called the Emory section included streets named for prestigious colleges, including Harvard, Oxford, Emory, and Cornell. Homes on Ridgecrest, Ridgewood and surrounding streets were built in the 1930s and 1940s. Emory Grove, a section of modest Cape Cod houses, was built in the late 1940s. The Parkwood section was developed in the mid-1950s. Homes appeared surrounding the new Fernbank School beginning in the early 1960s on Heaton Park Drive, Dyson Drive, Artwood Road, Hummingbird Lane, and other streets. Except for infill housing on vacant lots, the final subdivision built in Druid Hills was Durand Mill.

The Adair Realty Company reaped a fortune selling land and houses in Druid Hills. This ad appeared in the *Atlanta Journal* newspaper in 1922. (Courtesy of the *Atlanta Journal-Constitution*.)

Scenes in Druid Hills, Atlanta's Famous Residence Section

The *Atlanta Journal* newspaper printed "Scenes from Druid Hills" in 1923. It was used to advertise the new community and entice people to purchase homes there. (Courtesy of the *Atlanta Journal-Constitution*.)

The George Steffner family moved to "rural" Oakdale Road after being displaced by the Great Atlanta Fire in 1917, which swept through Old Fourth Ward. The lot was purchased in 1919, and the house was built in 1920. The Steffner family lived in the house for over 50 years. (Courtesy of George Ulrich Steffner III.)

This is the Ridgewood Road bungalow of the William Horne Jr. family. The photograph of the bungalow was taken in 1929. The Horne family owned the Horne Desk and Furniture company. William Horne Jr. married his neighbor Frankie Kopf. (Courtesy of Carol Horne.)

Two fairly new homes are lined up on Ridgeview Road, and landscaping appears to be underway. These homes exist today. Note the empty lot where a future home will be built. (Courtesy of Carol Horne.)

The By Way was a road cut in going east/west to allow the trolley to reach all the roads going north/south starting from Lullwater Road on the east end to Briarcliff Road on the west end. This home, belonging to the Coster family, was located on the By Way. Dorothy Coster married Leonard Dobson, and all the Dobson children were raised in the home. This photograph was taken in 1929. (Courtesy of Carolyn Dobson.)

Florrie Guy (left) and Allie Guy stand in the front yard of their home on North Decatur Road in front of their Pontiac automobile around the 1930s. (Courtesy of Helen McSwain.)

Sanborn maps were used by fire insurance companies to note the location and construction of various homes and buildings. This map covers Cornell Road, one of the College Streets. This one shows the words "Reserved for Druid Hills." This reserved land was proposed as a site for Druid Hills High School and is at the corner of Harvard Road and Emory Road. (Courtesy of the Atlanta History Center.)

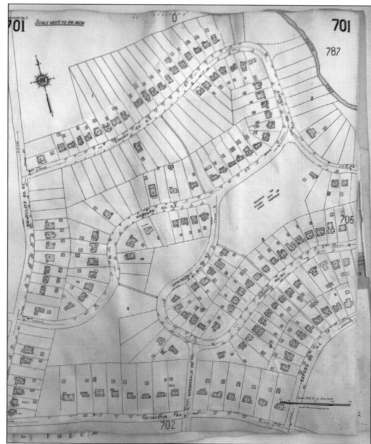

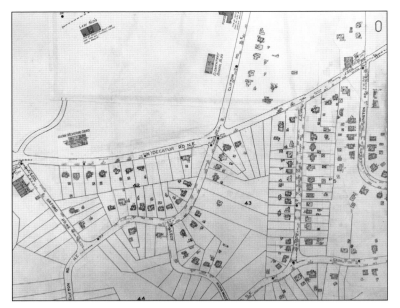

This Sanborn map shows Ridgewood Drive and University Drive, Northeast. University Drive was later named Emory Drive. (Courtesy of Atlanta History Center.)

Dr. Richard Sams grew up in this home (right) on North Decatur Road and later purchased the home from his family. He and his wife continue to live there. Dr. Sams is related to some of the oldest settlers in the Druid Hills area and is an author, historian, and geologist. (Courtesy of Richard Sams.)

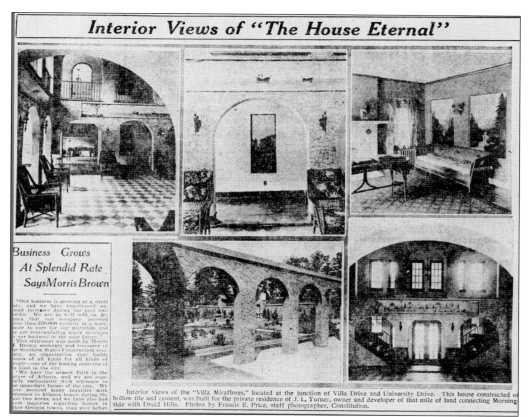

Interior Views of "The House Eternal"

Business Grows At Splendid Rate Says Morris Brown

"Our business is growing at a rapid rate, and we have experienced unusual increases during the past two weeks. We are so well and on Atlanta that our company invested more than $50,000 recently in a warehouse to care for our materials and we are contemplating heavy increases in our business in the near future."

This statement was made by Morris L. Brown, secretary and treasurer of the Southern States Construction company, an organization that builds homes of all kinds for all kinds of people—one of the leading concerns of its kind in the city.

"We have the utmost faith in the future of Atlanta, and we are especially enthusiastic with reference to the immediate future of the city. We have received many inquiries with reference to Atlanta homes during the last two weeks, and we have also had more inquiries regarding homes in other Georgia towns, than ever before

Interior views of the "Villa Miraflores," located at the junction of Villa Drive and University Drive. This house constructed of hollow tile and cement, was built for the private residence of J. L. Turner, owner and developer of that mile of land connecting Morningside with Druid Hills. Photos by Francis E. Price, staff photographer, Constitution.

Villa Drive was home to six houses, perched on a hill close to Buddie Candler's property at Briarcliff. The homes were designed by James Turner, with landscape design by Henry Jordan. The Mediterranean Revival style villas were built in 1925. The homes were advertised as being high quality, constructed of hollow tile, which would not burn or rust. The homes were constructed for the "man of moderate means." (*Atlanta Journal-Constitution*, April 24, 1919, courtesy of Sue Sullivan.)

Emory Highlands was developed in the early 1920s. This June 1923 ad is from the *Atlanta Constitution* and promotes lots on North Decatur Road, Burlington Road, and Emory Road. (Courtesy of the *Atlanta Journal-Constitution*.)

With the Sam Guy house in the background, the trolley tracks going up Oxford Road are visible. The house still stands and is a private residence. (Courtesy of Helen McSwain.)

Florrie and her father, Sam Guy, pose with their two dogs. The house in the background is the home of George Moore, who owned the George Moore Ice Cream Company. Sam Guy was a chemistry professor at Emory University. (Courtesy of Helen McSwain.)

The photograph above shows the home Dan Bodin designed and built for himself. The house is located on Springdale Road. A portrait of Dan Bodin is at right. Bodin was a famous architect who worked with Charles Frazier and designed and built Buddie Candler's Briarcliff Mansion. (Both, courtesy of Cris Connelly.)

This is an advertisement for homes and land on Cornell Road, one of the College Streets. The College Streets were named after prestigious universities by Walter Candler on land originally owned by Walter Candler. This 1924 photograph shows 3 Cornell Road. (Courtesy of Newspapers.com.)

This photograph shows a typical house on Cornell Road, one of the College Streets. The other College Streets are named after Harvard, Emory, and Oxford Universities. (Courtesy of Newspapers.com)

Dave and Barbara Franz stand in the backyard of their Tudor Revival home at 858 Springdale Road in 1949. (Courtesy of Emily Franz.)

Emerging from the Depression years, families with small children in Druid Hills commonly had domestic servants. They cooked, cleaned, washed clothes, and served as endearing caregivers. This 1937 photograph shows Nellie Smith in the yard of 1309 North Decatur Road, with the present owner, Dr. Richard Sams in the baby stroller. (Courtesy of Richard Sams.)

Neighborhood children attend a birthday party in the yard of the home of the Sewell family, located at 631 Clifton Road. The picture was taken in 1937. Note the various porters and maids in uniforms. (Courtesy of Tony Reeves and Jane Carey Armes.)

The majority of families living in Druid Hills had help that became a part of their family. This photograph shows Walt, an endeared part of the Candler / Guy family. Allie Candler was the daughter of Judge John Candler, who lived at the corner of Ponce de Leon and Briarcliff Road. She married Sam Guy and moved to North Decatur Road. The Guy home is still standing and is lived in by family members. (Courtesy of Helen McSwain.)

Marshall Kline grew up in this Tudor Revival home at 909 Oakdale Road. Kline is shown at his engagement party in the backyard of the home in 1942. (Courtesy of Marshall Kline.)

Marshall Kline (foreground) and two unidentified friends play in the backyard of 909 Oakdale Road near the garage of the home. Their domestic servant stands in the back doorway of the home. (Courtesy of Marshall Kline.)

Polly Paxton, childhood friend of Julia Ann Dobson, stands at the corner of Emory Circle and North Decatur Road around 1941. The home seen on the left is one of the oldest in Druid Hills. They were built before Asa Candler purchased the property. (Courtesy of Julia Ann Dobson.)

In 1940, Betty Mackay (later Asbury) was 12 years of age. From left to right are Margie Graf, Miriam Laughlin, Dorothy Quillian, Betty, Lena Maxcey, Rachel Stubbs, and Kathryn Graf. (Courtesy of Betty Mackay Asbury.)

This April 1926 advertisement solicits buyers for the New Clifton section. This section of Druid Hills stretched from Ponce De Leon north to the driveways of the Harrisons and Hodgsons, who lived in Fernbank Forest. After these two driveways, Clifton Road was a dirt road. (Courtesy of the *Atlanta Journal*.)

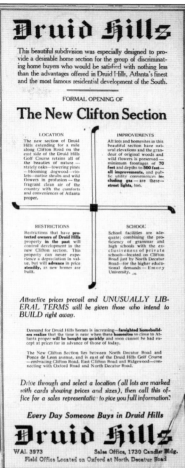

Druid Hills

This beautiful subdivision was especially designed to provide a desirable home section for the group of discriminating home buyers who would be satisfied with nothing less than the advantages offered in Druid Hills, Atlanta's finest and the most famous residential development of the South.

FORMAL OPENING OF

The New Clifton Section

LOCATION
The new section of Druid Hills extending for a mile along Clifton Road on the east side of the Druid Hills Golf Course retains all of the beauties of nature — stately oaks — towering pines — blooming dogwood — violets — native shrubs and wild flowers in profusion — the fragrant clean air of the country with the comforts and conveniences of Atlanta proper.

IMPROVEMENTS
All lots and homesites in this beautiful section have natural elevations and the grandeur of original woods and wild flowers is preserved — minimum frontages of 70 feet and depths to 500 feet — **all improvements**, and public utility conveniences including gas — are there — **street lights, too.**

RESTRICTIONS
Restrictions that have **protected owners of Druid Hills property in the past** will control development in the new Clifton section. This property can never experience a depreciation in value, but will **advance in price steadily**, as new homes are built.

SCHOOL
School facilities are adequate; combining the proficiency of grammar and high schools with the exclusiveness of private schools—located on Clifton Road just by North Decatur Road—for the higher educational demands — Emory University.

Attractive prices prevail and UNUSUALLY LIBERAL TERMS will be given those who intend to BUILD right away.

Demand for Druid Hills homes is increasing—**farsighted homebuilders realize** that the time is near when these homesites so close to Atlanta proper **will be bought up quickly** and soon cannot be had except at prices far in advance of those of today.

The New Clifton Section lies between North Decatur Road and Ponce de Leon avenue, and is east of the Druid Hills Golf Course—embracing Clifton Road, East Clifton Road and Ridgewood—connecting with Oxford Road and North Decatur Road.

Drive through and select a location (all lots are marked with cards showing prices and sizes), then call this office for a sales representative to give you full information.

Every Day Someone Buys in Druid Hills

Druid Hills

WAl. 3973   Sales Office, 1730 Candler Bldg.
Field Office Located on Oxford at North Decatur Road

This shows the construction of an apartment building on North Decatur Road in the 1930s. The apartments were to house Emory faculty and employees and were designed by Neal Smith. These apartments no longer stand. (Courtesy of Sue Sullivan.)

This photograph shows an advertisement for Emory Grove, which included Princeton Way, Edinburgh Terrace, and Westminster Way, as well as homes on North Decatur Road. Neal Smith was head of maintenance for Emory and later designed the Snapper lawn mower. (Courtesy of Sue Sullivan.)

Princeton Way was a street within the Emory Grove section of Druid Hills—located on the south side of North Decatur Road. These streets were developed from 1939 to 1942 as affordable housing. (Courtesy of Sue Sullivan.)

Westminster Way was a part of the Emory Grove development. This shot was taken in 1947. What made Emory Grove unique were the pocket parks behind the homes. These hidden parks included picnic pavilions and tennis courts. (Courtesy of Robert Gerwig.)

Three boys stand in a yard on Westminster Way around 1957. From left to right are unidentified, Billy Warkinton, and Robert Gerwig. (Courtesy of Robert Gerwig.)

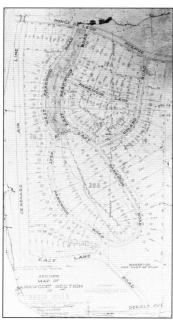

This is a map of the Parkwoods neighborhood, which was built between 1948 and 1960.

This midcentury modern furniture was inside a home on Parkwood Road. Most of the Parkwood section was constructed in the late 1940s to 1950s. Ranch homes were popular, but other architectural styles also existed. In-fill housing was built on vacant lots as late as the 1970s. Parkwood had its own garden club, which became defunct in the 1960s but has been revived by current residents. (Courtesy of Parkwood Garden Club.)

From left to right, Don, Del, and Charles Wynn are pictured at their home on Heaton Park Drive in the 1960s. Heaton Park was part of the Chelsea Heights Section built between 1957 and 1962.

This picture shows a scene from Dyson Drive, which intersected with East Clifton Road. Other streets in this Chelsea Heights section of Druid Hills include Coventry Road, Vickers Drive and Circle, Chelsea Road, and Heaton Park Drive. Pictured is Doug Grimm's 1950 Oldsmobile Rocket 88 hardtop convertible purchased in 1958. (Courtesy of Doug Grimm.)

This photograph shows a scene on Artwood Road. Artwood is an access road to the original Fernbank Elementary School, which was on Heaton Park Drive. Artwood Road, built between 1957 and 1962, had upscale ranch-type homes. Many professionals lived there. It had easy access to Fernbank School. (Courtesy of Sue Sullivan.)

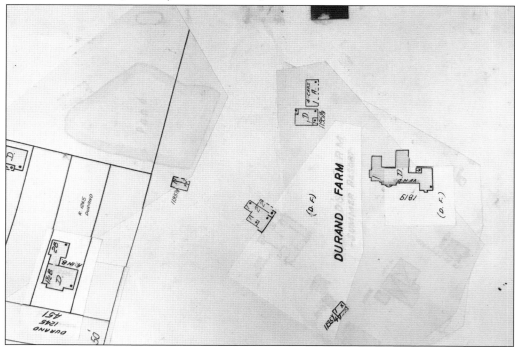

This section of a Sanborn map from the 1930s shows the Durand Farm, a 36-acre property used as a dairy. The Druid Hills Civic Association tried to raise money to purchase the property as a nature preserve but was unsuccessful. Durand Mill Subdivision was built on the property in 1992.

Five

SCHOOLS, PARKS, AND CHURCHES

The Emory School began in 1919 in Emory's Fishburne Building. In 1928, Louis Edmund Crook designed a new building for Druid Hills School, and it was built on Haygood Drive. Druid Hills Elementary was on the same campus as Druid Hills High until it moved to Fernbank School in 1959. Druid Hills had additions throughout the years: including a new gym, band room, library, and cafeteria. In 1969, the last white class graduated. In 1970, Druid Hills and Hamilton (an African American high school) merged. In 1971, the private Paideia School began in one Druid Hills mansion. Paideia now has numerous historic mansions and new buildings. Schools for special-needs children and adults came to Druid Hills, including the Howard School, Ben Franklin Academy, and the Cerebral Palsy Center School. The public Springdale Park School is in a former Neel Reid house and the Turner/Wein house and built several additions. With donations of 75 acres and $1 million from Asa Candler, a new university was formed from Oxford College of Emory, and the university moved to Druid Hills in 1915. Today, it is situated on over 600 acres and consists of nine divisions: Oxford College of Emory, the Graduate School, the Schools of Arts and Sciences, Business, Law, Medicine, Nursing, Public Health, and Theology. Emory owns or is affiliated with many organizations including the Carter Center, Yerkes Primate Center, the Centers for Disease Control and Prevention, Winship Cancer Center, Wesley Woods, and Emory and Children's Healthcare. Parks within Druid Hills include the Olmsted Linear Park, Burbanck Park, Rutledge Park, the Lullwater Conservation Garden, the Lullwater Preserve, and the Heaton Park Bird Sanctuary. Druid Hills has one private club, Druid Hills Golf Club, chartered in 1912. It is home to DeKalb County Schools' Fernbank Science Center, and Fernbank Museum of Natural History. Fernbank Forest, Hahn Woods, and Frazer Forest are old-growth woodlands. There are 10 religious organizations in Druid Hills: Atlanta Primitive Baptist, Jackson Hill and Druid Hills Baptist, Episcopal Church of the Epiphany, St. Elias Antiochian Orthodox Church, Emory and Druid Hills Presbyterian, Church of Jesus Christ of Latter-day Saints, St. John Lutheran, St. John Chrysostom Melkite Catholic Church, Glenn Memorial United Methodist, and the International Society for Krishna Consciousness (ISKCON). Druid Hills United Methodist Church merged with another church, and their property was sold for condominium development.

This photograph shows Glenn Memorial Church (with steeple) and Sunday school building (behind Glenn). The Emory Business Administration school is to the left rear of the church. The corner where South Oxford and North Decatur Roads intersect is empty. This lot was where Burns' Service Station later moved. Note the row of houses (some of which are gone) above the Burns' lot. (Courtesy of Rose Library at Emory University.)

This aerial view of Emory University's campus was taken in the 1930s. Wesley Memorial Hospital (Emory University Hospital) is in the left-bottom corner. The Emory Clinic is in the middle center. Andrews Circle (which no longer exists) is in the rear of the clinic buildings. In the distant background, Candler Lake can be viewed, and to the left of the lake, in the wooded area atop a hill, is Lullwater House. (Courtesy of Rose Library at Emory University.)

The trolley is turned around on Oxford Road and headed back to town (near the old Horton's Store.) This photograph shows trolley No. 617. The operator is talking to two brothers from Avondale Estates, Georgia. Steve Dean is in the argyle sweater, and his brother is Joe Dean. (Courtesy of Rose Library at Emory University.)

This is a photograph of a house at the corner of Clifton and North Decatur Roads. The Emory Law School is now located at this site. The stucco house was, at one time, the W.D. Thompson home. Thompson was a lawyer to Asa Candler and, later, dean of the Emory Law School. W.D. Thompson later moved to Springdale Road and deeded this house to Emory.

Starting in 1919, the Fishburne building at Emory was where the original Emory School for Druid Hills residents was held. It stood close to the corner of Clifton Road and North Decatur Road. It was later used as offices for Emory. It is no longer standing, and the Goizueta Business School is on the site. (Courtesy of Rose Library at Emory University.)

Druid Hills High School was built in 1928. The school was designed by Louis Edmund Crook and built by Harry J. Carr Construction Co. The school originally housed elementary through 11th grade. Today, it is one of the oldest public schools in DeKalb County. (Courtesy of June Rowan.)

This 1928 photograph shows Druid Hills High School's western entrance with Sue Mozely's class of elementary students. Note the debris at the bottom of the photograph—the school had just recently been completed, but construction refuse had not yet been cleaned up. (Courtesy of June Rowan.)

This is the third-grade class in 1944 at Druid Hills Elementary School, which was then a part of the high school campus. Richard Sams is pictured with his fellow classmates. (Courtesy of Dr. Richard Sams.)

A sign in front of Druid Hills High School, on the Haygood Road side, reads, "Emory University, Georgia." The post office and train depot also had that designation. Later, the name was dropped, and Emory was just a part of DeKalb County but had its own phone exchange and zip code. Emory University was later annexed into the City of Atlanta. (Courtesy of Rose Library at Emory University.)

The Out of Doors School was held in the backyard of Antoinette Johnson Matthews at 1097 Oakdale Road. This was the former site of the Johnson farm. The school operated from 1930 to the 1980s. Here, children at the school enjoy the playground. Matthews wrote the book *Oakdale Road* about the homes and residents of the street. (Courtesy of the Matthews family.)

Each student who attended the Out of Doors School received a certificate like the one pictured, certifying them as being ready to enter first grade in public school. The fee for the Out of Doors School was 25¢ per child per week. (Courtesy of Dick Diamond.)

THE OUT-OF-DOORS SCHOOL

THIS CERTIFIES THAT *Dicky Diamond*

HAS ATTENDED **THE OUT-OF-DOORS SCHOOL** FOR *4 years*

HAS ACHIEVED THE PROPER HABITS, ATTITUDES AND SKILLS. HAS ATTAINED THE REQUIRED AGE. BEEN IMMUNIZED FROM SMALL POX, DIPTHERIA AND TYPHOID. IS READY FOR *first grade* AND IS ENTITLED TO THIS

CERTIFICATE

ATLANTA, GEORGIA,
May 31 1946

Antonette Johnson Matthews
Elsie Wagnon Johnson R.N.

MRS. BAGWELL'S HOME

DANCING SCHOOL

Ar'lyn Worth School was located on south Oxford Road in Emory Village and first served children with special needs. Later, it became an after-school daycare. Dorothy Bagwell had earlier held dancing lessons for children with cerebral palsy at the same location. The Dutch Colonial home still stands. (Courtesy of Rose Library at Emory University.)

Fernbank Elementary School was named after Fernbank Forest. It was built in 1959 and served the community until the mid-2010s. The original Fernbank School was demolished in the mid-2010s and was replaced by a new school also known as Fernbank. Across the street is the Fernbank Science Center, a unit of DeKalb County Schools.

Glenn Memorial Methodist Church (later Glenn Memorial United Methodist Church) is newly constructed in this 1931 photograph. Philip Shutze designed the church. Flora Glenn Candler gave money to construct the church in memory of her father, Rev. Wilbur Fisk Glenn. (Courtesy of Rose Library at Emory University.)

Neal Smith designed the Sunday school building of Glenn Memorial. Inside the building, Philip Shutze designed a magnificent "Little Chapel" based upon Saint Stephen Wallbrook, London, designed by Sir Christopher Wren. (Courtesy of Rose Library at Emory University.)

Rev. E.G. Mackay was a Methodist minister who served several churches in the community, including Druid Hills Methodist and Glenn Memorial Methodist. He was active in all aspects of the Methodist Church and helped acquire Cane Creek Falls for Camp Glisson—a Methodist Camp—from its Druid Hills owner, Preston Arkwright. (Courtesy of Betty Mackay Asbury.)

Flora Glenn Candler donated the money to build a parsonage for Glenn Memorial Methodist Church. The house, located on Clifton Road near North Decatur Road, was the residence for pastors of Glenn. It was designed by Philip Shutze. Pictured from left to right are one of Betty Mackay Asbury's brothers, the family dog, and Betty's mother. (Courtesy of Betty Mackay Asbury.)

In its heyday, Druid Hills Baptist Church was the largest Baptist church in the southeast. Dr. Louie DeVotie Newton was its long-term and famous pastor. Dr. Newton was known as "Mr. Baptist." The church, at the corner of North Highland and Ponce de Leon Avenues, was designed by Edward E. Dougherty in 1914. The two buildings facing Ponce de Leon are original, and the building at far right rear-facing Highland was added later. (Courtesy of Druid Hills Baptist Church.)

Pastor Louie Newton, of the Druid Hills Baptist Church, meets Jimmy and Roslyn Carter in this photograph. The occasion is unknown. The Newtons lived on Oakdale Road at Number 1011, where Dr. Newton had cows and goats in his backyard. (Courtesy of Druid Hills Baptist Church.)

A group of orphans from the Baptist children's home arrives at Druid Hills Baptist Church for a holiday dinner and Christmas celebration. Across Ponce de Leon, some of the homes that remain standing are visible. (Courtesy of Druid Hills Baptist Church.)

Hovie Lister was a Baptist gospel singer and pianist who performed with his musical group, the Statesmen. Lister was a regular at Druid Hills Baptist, where he was frequently a performer. Lister also served as a deacon at the church. (Courtesy of Druid Hills Baptist Church.)

The Druid Hills Presbyterian Church was founded in 1883 as the Fourth Presbyterian Church in downtown Atlanta. It was designed by Francis Palmer Smith. The Sunday school building was built in 1923, and the sanctuary was built in 1939. It remains an active congregation today.

A lovely home on Fairview Road was the parsonage for the Druid Hills Presbyterian Church. In this photograph, men pose after raking leaves and doing yard work in the front yard of the home. From left to right are A.T. Thompson, Austin Dilbeck, Jim Graff, T.O. Andrew, Guy Mayes, Jack Holt, Bob McFarland, George Allen, and J.A. Hickman. (Courtesy of Sue Sullivan.)

The Druid Hills Methodist Church was designed by Ivey and Crook in 1955 and constructed on the former site of Judge John Candler's home. In 1982, the Druid Hills Preschool was established there. The family of John Candler retained ownership of the iron fence surrounding the property throughout all subsequent changes in ownership. The Ponce de Leon property was sold, and condominiums were built inside the existing structures.

Emory Presbyterian Church began as a mission of Decatur Presbyterian. It was constructed in the Gothic style in 1947 at the corner of Haygood Road and North Decatur Road. A labyrinth was added in 2002. It remains an active congregation.

Six

BUSINESSES, INSTITUTIONS, AND ORGANIZATIONS

The premier and most historic shopping district in Druid Hills is known as Emory Village and dates from the 1920s. In years past, it contained a hardware store, jewelers, restaurants, gas stations, beauty parlors, dance studios, an after-school daycare, flower shops, bowling alley, drugstores, grocery stores, a movie theater, and dry cleaners. As Druid Hills has grown, stores in Emory Village have changed hands many times, and several new strip malls have been build or redeveloped nearby.

Organizations affiliated with and located within Druid Hills are the Druid Hills and Lullwater Garden Clubs, both founded in 1928. Both clubs sent delegates to Athens, Georgia, to help form the Garden Club of Georgia. The Druid Hills Garden Club adopted Olmsted's Oak Grove Park and built a memorial fountain there, as well as gardens, and it continues to this day to plant dogwood trees in the park in memory of deceased members. The Lullwater Garden Club owns the Lullwater Conservation Garden, a six-acre woodland and meadow filled with six champion trees (and one Georgia State champion) and planted with many native plants. The conservation garden is a certified wildlife refuge, Audubon Bird Sanctuary, and a member of the Old Growth Forest Network. The Druid Hills Civic Association (DHCA) was founded in 1938 and continues to this day. The organization's prime source of income is its popular annual tour of homes and gardens. When formed, DHCA's goals were, "working to preserve the unique character of this neighborhood and the sense of community of its residents; historic preservation, environmental conservation, advocacy causes and community events." CAUTION, Inc.—which stands for Coalition Against Unnecessary Thoroughfares in Older Neighborhoods—was formed for in 1982 the sole purpose of fighting the expressway proposed to bisect Druid Hills and the linear park. The Olmsted Parks Society of Atlanta was formed in 1983 to educate the public about Olmsted, and to fight the proposed expressway. Roadbusters, founded in 1985, was a grassroots organization that fought the road via acts of peaceful noncooperation and protest. Many of its members went to jail in the service of protesting the road. The Olmsted Linear Park Alliance was formed in 1997 to raise money for a master plan to direct the renovation of the linear park and execute that master plan. The renovation was accomplished by raising over $10 million and through a coalition of public and private agencies. Today, the linear park looks much as it did when Olmsted designed it.

The Emory University, Georgia Post Office was located at the corner of Clifton Road and Haygood Road. Later, Emory University, Georgia went away in favor of Atlanta, Georgia. Emory was officially annexed into the City of Atlanta in 2018. Constructed in the early 1920s, the building also housed (at different times) a barbershop, a shoe-shine stand, and a drugstore. (Courtesy of Sue Sullivan.)

This photograph shows a different view of the post office. Ivey's Drugstore was next door, which was a good location near Emory University Hospital. Ivey's had a lunch counter inside which was a popular place for Emory employees to eat. (Courtesy of Rose Library at Emory University.)

Emory Village was the main shopping district of Emory. The village was located at the intersections of South Oxford, North Decatur, and Oxford Roads. In this image, all the buildings to the left of the Gulf truck were destroyed in a fire during the 1970s. (Courtesy of Rose Library at Emory University.)

This photograph shows another view of Emory Village. The land for the village was donated to Emory by Asa Candler. Shops were built first along South Oxford and, later, at the east end of North Decatur Road. (Courtesy of the Rose Library at Emory University.)

In the early days of the village, it contained myriad businesses. This aerial shot of the stores includes service stations, grocery stores, a hardware store, a radio store, a florist, two dry cleaners, several restaurants, a movie theater, and a bowling alley. (Courtesy of Rose Library at Emory University.)

These ads from the 1951 *Saga* yearbook advertise some of the businesses that were located in Emory Village. The *Saga* was the school annual of Druid Hills High School. (Courtesy of Sue Sullivan.)

HORTON'S

DRUG

STORE

In The Village

☆

The Convenient Place

To Meet

The official name of Horton's Dry Good Store was the Shop 'N Basket, but Druid Hills residents always called it Horton's after the owners' last name. Patrons could buy just about anything at Horton's. In fact, there was a sign in the window that said, "If we don't have it, you don't need it." Horton's had a lunch counter and a jukebox. Horton's was on Oxford Road, and the business has closed. (Courtesy of Rose Library at Emory University.)

Oliver's Emory Drugs was a pharmacy located at the end of the North Decatur Road row of shops in Emory Village. It was a handy place to go for having a prescription filled. It was in the same location as the former Jeffaires and Giles' Drug Stores. A Super Cuts occupies the space now. This photograph shows Dr. Robert Oliver, who was the father of Rep. Mary Margaret Oliver of the Georgia House of Representatives. (Courtesy of Rose Library at Emory University.)

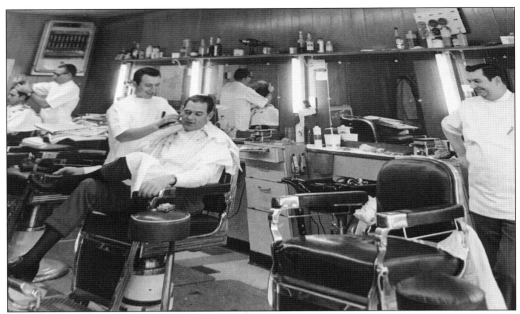

There was a barbershop located in Emory Village, right next to the Emory Theatre. One of the barbers was Willie Noon (left), and another was Harold Garett (right.) After the Emory Village fire, the shop moved next to Horton's. The photograph was taken in 1971. (Courtesy of Sue Sullivan.)

Druid Hills had its own fire service. Here, two trucks are parked in front of the station on North Decatur Road. Unfortunately, if one did not subscribe to the fire service and pay a fee, the firemen would not come to the fire. Older residents recount stories of homes burning to the ground while neighbors and volunteer firemen watched. (Courtesy of Sue Sullivan.)

These neighborhood boys are standing in front of the Druid Hills Fire Station in the 1940s. A Pure Oil gas station is in the background. The boys are (from left to right) Bill Tatum, Don Waddington, Oliver Sale, Connor Nelson, and Steve Harrington. (Courtesy of Sue Sullivan.)

MEETS SECOND MONDAY NIGHT IN EACH MONTH

H. T. Dobbs, Pres.
1073 Oakdale Road, N. E.

D. C. Jones, Jr., Sec'y
1367 Springdale Road, N. E.

DRUID HILLS CIVIC ASSOCIATION
Promoting Community Progress

June 1, 1939

TO THE RESIDENTS OF DRUID HILLS:

In presenting this Directory to you, we know you will realize and appreciate more fully the surroundings in which you live. Your neighbors, like you, are having things brought out in the open and discussed which you have wondered about for a long time. In this Directory are names of 1,500 Druid Hills residents. There are about 1,100 homes, of which 900 are occupied by owners.

The Druid Hills Civic Association is now six months old and we have 360 members. Look through your Directory—CA designates a member of the Association. A great many of the most active and interested citizens have already joined. If you are not a member, send your name and $1.00 to the Chairman of the Membership Committee, Mrs. Clyde King, Jr., 1062 Lullwater Road, N. E., or to the Secretary.

The Association has accomplished a lot—our main activities right now are property restrictions and water costs.

Come to the meetings the second Monday night of each month at eight o'clock at the school auditorium and bring your neighbors. You can help make this a progressive community. By active cooperation of all, we will stand out above all sections in the southeast. Divided we disintegrate, united we stand.

We need your last two months water bills in connection with a proposed water system. Send them to your Secretary.

Sincerely,

D. C. JONES, JR., Secretary.

DCJ:SJ

The Druid Hills Civic Association was founded in 1938 when the original covenants ran out on Druid Hills property. The group wanted fire coverage, water, and better educational facilities as well as other civic goals. The group published the *Druid Hills News*. This photo shows the opening page of the 1939 DHCA directory. (Courtesy of Sue Sullivan.)

A group of boy scouts from Troop 18, sponsored by Glenn Memorial Methodist Church, ride in a truck with their equipment taking them to a campsite at Camp Big Heart in Pensacola, Florida, in 1948. The donor was a member of the troop, which celebrates its 100th anniversary in 2022. (Courtesy of Richard Sams.)

Boy Scouts from Troop 18 stand at their booth on North Decatur Road. They sold drinks for 5¢. Pictured from left to right are Sam Guy, Walter Calhoun, unidentified, and Billy White. Sam Massell (later a mayor of Atlanta) also sold drinks at a booth. (Courtesy of Helen McSwain.)

Emily Harrison had this Girl Scout cabin built inside Fernbank Forest. "Miss Emily" often let local scout troops use the Fernbank property for camping and nature skills training. The Harrison family's house, "Fernbank," was also used for classes. (Courtesy of Rose Library at Emory University.)

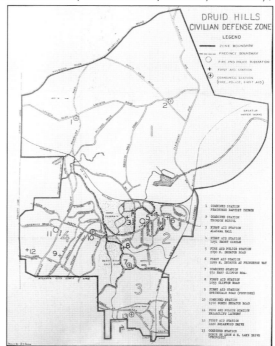

During World War II, Druid Hills had its own civil defense plan. Depending upon where you lived, you evacuated to a different location in case of emergency or disaster. (Courtesy of Rose Library at Emory University.)

A Victory Garden was planted by neighbors in the Emory Grove section of Druid Hills during World War II. The garden was in the interior park back of homes that fronted on Princeton Way. (Courtesy of Sue Sullivan.)

Claude Burns, owner of Burns Service Station, escorts two children across South Oxford Road in Druid Hills. (Courtesy of Rose Library at Emory University.)

The number six Emory bus went from Emory Grove to downtown Atlanta. In this photograph, the bus is boarding passengers at a covered bus stop near Emory Presbyterian Church (in rear) and Druid Hills High School. The bus is going west on North Decatur Road. Houses in Emory Grove can be seen in the background on the right. (Courtesy of Sue Sullivan.)

The Lullwater Garden Club was chartered in 1928 as one of the first garden clubs in Georgia. This view is of the Lullwater Conservation Garden. Lullwater is one of the few clubs that owned its own garden—this one is six-and-a-half acres. This view is of the meadow just past the formal entrance off of Lullwater Road. In the background are homes on the east side of Lullwater Road. (Courtesy of the Lullwater Garden Club.)

This set of stone pillars designates the beginning of the native plant garden in the Lullwater Conservation Garden. The garden club has been taking care of the garden since 1939 and purchased it from Emory in 1961. (Courtesy of Lullwater Garden Club.)

The members of the Druid Hills Garden Club were caretakers of Oak Grove Park beginning in 1928. They erected this memorial stone fountain to honor deceased members and their relatives and built a rose garden and walking paths. These elements were removed as part of the renovation of the linear park. The club continues to plant dogwood trees in memory of deceased members.

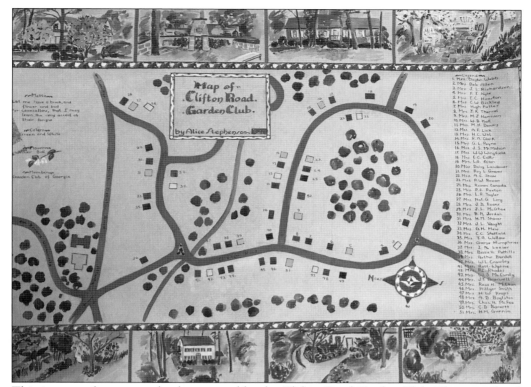

This is a page from a scrapbook preserved by the Clifton Road Garden Club. The map, dated 1945, is hand painted and shows the homes of all the members. There were a great number of garden clubs. (Courtesy of the Clifton Road Garden Club.)

Officers of the Princeton Way Garden Club are pictured in 1949–1950. Princeton Way was part of Emory Grove neighborhood. (Courtesy of the Princeton Road Garden Club.)

This home, in Fernbank Forest, was named Fernbank. It was the home of Col. Zadock Harrison and family. Daughter Emily Harrison is responsible for preserving the forest and saving it from development. Fernbank Museum of Natural History and Fernbank Science Center were all visions of "Miss Emily." (Courtesy of Rose Library at Emory University.)

Fernbank was a large expanse of old-growth forest. In its midst was a pond where the Harrison children played, swam, and fished. Near the pond was a huge rock outcropping known as "Elephant Rock." (Courtesy of Rose Library at Emory University.)

The Emory University Women's Club met in this rock building near the intersection of Haygood Road and Clifton Road. The house no longer stands. (Courtesy of Rose Library at Emory University.)

The Druid Hills Golf Course Clubhouse was constructed in 1912–1913 from plans drawn by Edward E. Dougherty. Although Dougherty called for brick and slate, the club cut corners by using clapboard and composition roofing. In 1925, the clubhouse burned down, while golfers continued to play as the embers flew around them. The Druid Hills Golf Club was chartered in 1912 as a private gentlemen's club. The 18-hole golf course was designed by H.H. Barker. President of Georgia Power, H.M. Atkinson was the first president. Bobby Jones won the first club championship at the age of 14.

After the clapboard, Druid Hills Golf Club clubhouse burned in 1925, it was rebuilt using Dougherty's original plan, except this time, the builders used brick and slate, as Dougherty had originally specified. Today, the golf club thrives with full membership, tennis and golf programs, a swim team, exercise programs, and excellent restaurants. The club hosts an amateur golf tournament known as the Dogwood Invitational. The club was the scene of most social affairs in Druid Hills, from weddings to tea dances, to banquets, to performances by the Metropolitan Opera singers during Atlanta's Opera Week, to a visit by US president Warren G. Harding.

In January 1979, a grease fire at Dawgwood's Sandwich Shop spread to the roofs of nearby buildings. From the Emory Theatre down to just before the old Everybody's Pizza Restaurant, all of the buildings along south Oxford Road were destroyed. (Courtesy of Sue Trowbridge.)

DeKalb County Firemen fight the blaze at Emory Village and attempt to save additional buildings from the fire. In the subfreezing weather, water from fire hoses froze on the street. (Courtesy of Sue Trowbridge.)

The Emory Pines Inn was a motel on North Decatur Road that served visitors to Emory University. The Clifton Condominium building was erected on the site after the Emory Pines Inn was demolished.

Built in 1967, the Fernbank Science Center is part of the DeKalb County School District. It has various exhibits of a scientific nature, a planetarium, and a giant telescope.

The CDC has had several name changes through the years. This is the Communicable Disease Center Building One (the first one built on CDC property and the first one razed), constructed in 1960 on 15 wooded acres on Clifton Road and since demolished. Coca-Cola magnate Robert Woodruff assisted Emory in acquiring the center. CDC later became the Centers for Disease Control and the words "and Prevention" were added later. The CDCs publication, *Morbidity and Mortality Weekly Report*, first mentioned what would later be known as AIDS/HIV in 1981. The CDC led a 15-year effort to vaccinate humans against smallpox, which led to the global eradication of the disease in 1977. (Courtesy of the Sensor Museum at the CDC.)

Seven

THE DECLINE
OF DRUID HILLS

Many factors contributed to the decline of Druid Hills. Some date the decline as early as 1943, when the neighborhood was shocked and terrified by the murder of Henry Heinz. Others say that the decline began when owners of the great estates and mansions moved to Buckhead, a rich, up-and-coming neighborhood. Finding buyers for the huge homes in Druid Hills was difficult, and the historic structures required maintenance. Many were turned into boardinghouses or rental houses. Finally, the Georgia Department of Transportation's plans for an expressway through the neighborhood caused many residents to sell and move elsewhere. It seemed no one wanted to live in a neighborhood cut in half by a strip of concrete. In addition, Ponce de Leon Avenue was zoned A-L, which stood for "Apartment-Limited," and A-L allowed high-rise buildings along the street. Without covenants, and without historic district zoning or a Landmark District designation, homes could be demolished and were, often being replaced by condominiums or several houses on the lot where a mansion had once stood. A once-beautiful garden was considered an empty piece of land to build upon. Some homes became rental property and had absentee landlords, and the houses were not maintained. As a result, many homes in Druid Hills suffered from neglect.

The former Harris home, located at the corner of South Ponce de Leon (No. 1509) and Ponce de Leon, was in a decrepit state when it was purchased for classrooms for the newly formed Paideia School in 1970. (Courtesy of the Paideia School.)

Children from the Paideia School are hard at work clearing brush and debris from the yard of the house that became the school's first building, now known as the 1509 Building. (Courtesy of the Paideia School.)

In the beginning, Paideia was a small school with a modest enrollment. Today, the school has several blocks of new buildings and historic mansions, and its enrollment is quite large. This photograph shows a Paideia school class sitting on the second memorial fountain that was first built by the Druid Hills Garden Club. (Courtesy of the Paideia School.)

Pinebloom was the palatial mansion of Preston Arkwright, president of the Georgia Power Company and the Atlanta Street Railway Company. Arkwright coined the phrase "A Citizen wherever we serve" for the power company and was an early proponent of hydroelectric power. The Jackson Hill Baptist Church is the building connected to the house.

Because they could not afford the upkeep, the Jackson Hill Baptist Church donated the entire Pinebloom estate to the Georgia Baptist Mission Board. During the 1990s and 2000s, the board did no maintenance on the church building or carriage house but did maintain the Pinebloom mansion. The carriage house is shown here in vandalized and deplorable condition. Pinebloom will be turned into condominiums.

El Paradisio was owned by absentee landlords, and no maintenance was done on it for decades. After it was no longer rentable, it was left empty and standing open. The grounds became a dumping area for refuse. Soon, glass was broken, and doors in the home were broken down. This photograph dates from 1973.

The once fine and beautiful mansion had greenhouses, servants' quarters, and a sunken Japanese tea garden—all left to ruin throughout several decades. The owners apparently hoped to sell the exquisite home for development. As time passed, everything of value was stripped from the house including doors, toilets, and walnut paneling. This photograph was taken in 1973. After years of decay and ruin and a fire that collapsed the roof, the City of Atlanta demolished the house. Today, it is the site of the Paradiso Condominiums. (Note that the original name of the house was changed.)

This photograph is taken in the entrance hall in front of the circular staircase in El Paradisio, looking toward the front door. There is broken glass, and the front door is damaged. Before long, the fabulous home would be a complete ruin. After years of decay and ruin, and a fire that collapsed the roof, the City of Atlanta demolished El Paradisio. Today, it is the site of Condominiums.

Even the bridges in Druid Hills are beautiful. This photograph, taken in the early 1970s, shows the arched concrete supports holding up the bridge on Ponce de Leon that traverses Lullwater Creek. One resident calls the site "Engulfed Cathedral."

Rainbow Terrace, the home built for Lucy Candler Heinz, was abandoned by her after the murder of her husband in the library. This photograph was taken in 1973. The house was left open and subject to vandalism and ruin.

After changing hands a few times, Rainbow Terrace was eventually abandoned. It was left open and suffered from vandalism and neglect. It was occasionally used as a site for filming horror movies. It was also a dumping place for trash. This photograph was taken in 1973.

Everything that could be pried up and removed from Rainbow Terrace was stolen. Eventually, the mansion was broken into condominiums, and a large number of new condominiums were built around the mansion. Architect Lloyd Preacher usually added a child's playhouse to the yards of his designs. This was the playhouse for Rainbow Terrace. It was demolished when the mansion was converted to condominiums.

Briarcliff estate was purchased by the US government as a site for a Veteran's Administration Hospital, which was never built there. Later, the State of Georgia bought the property as an alcohol treatment center and constructed the Georgia Mental Health Institute (GMHI) there. Buddie Candler's terraces and greenhouses were where a giant parking lot now exists.

After GMHI closed, the Briarcliff Estate was bought by Emory University. At first, Emory used some of the buildings, but by 2018, most were abandoned or used for storage of excess property. This photograph shows the ruins of the swimming pool.

The public does not know what Emory plans to do with the former GMHI tower and the cottages that surround it. Briarcliff Mansion has been virtually abandoned, and Emory has not maintained the home even though it is listed in the National Register of Historic Places. This photograph was taken in 2018.

The Georgia Mental Health Center is occasionally used for horror films or, as in 2016, the filming of *Stranger Things*.

The gardens of the Cator Woolford estate still exist. The Cerebral Palsy Center School occupied the house after the Woolfords sold it. They later built a school building on the rear of the property. Today, the home is used as the Atlanta Hospitality House, a place where relatives of those in area hospitals can stay for a small fee. This photograph shows two children from the school in front of the former mansion. (Courtesy of Atlanta Hospital Hospitality House.)

The Cerebral Palsy Center and School changed its name to the REACH center and served special needs children and adults under 6 and over 18. Two employees of the school—Herman White, porter, and Laura Colby, maid—help students John Brandenburg, left, and Susan Morton, right, raise the American flag in this photograph. (Courtesy of Atlanta Hospital Hospitality House.)

Today, the Cerebral Palsy Center School and REACH are called the Frazer Center, and they continue to serve special-needs individuals. Cator Woolford's mansion is used as the Atlanta Hospitality House. The picture shows the stairwell in the home. (Courtesy of Sue Sullivan.)

Remnants of the old Venable Mansion still exist. The interior of the mansion, Stonehenge, is shopworn, as seen in this interior photograph. This is a carved wooden monk. The basement is filled with similar carving. Today, the St. John Lutheran Church, which owns the property, is renovating the home. (Courtesy of Sue Sullivan.)

Forrest Adair did not live in his large home very long—he moved to a smaller house. The residence changed hands many times and then became a boardinghouse.

The George Adair estate, called the Villa, later became a boardinghouse for business women known as the Lullwater Club Residences. Mary Engle sits on the steps of the club with her dog in the 1960s. (Courtesy of Darin Engle.)

This brochure for the Lullwater Club Residences outlines the various amenities offered. After the boardinghouse closed, the property was sold for development. Bulldozers and a wrecking ball demolished the Villa. The Lion's Gate Condominiums were built on the site. (Courtesy of Darin Engle.)

Beautiful Grounds resembling a large estate or country club — Badminton court, lighted at night — Lovely lawn for sun bathing — Free parking area for automobiles

Good Public Transportation, bus stops in front of premises — Twenty to thirty minutes from downtown business center

Walking Distance of community center, theater and four churches — About one and a half miles of Emory University and Hospital

Very Reasonable monthly rates for permanent guests — Rates that girls regularly employed in banks, offices, department stores and teachers can afford — Also reasonable transient rates for visiting and temporary guests

Management: Trained, experienced and capable matrons with assistance of colored cooks, maids, butler, et. al.

REFERENCES REQUIRED

For Further Information Write or Call

Resident Manager

TELEPHONE NUMBER: DEarborn 0822

The South's Finest Club
**Residence For Business
And Professional Girls**

THE LULLWATER CLUB RESIDENCE
Established 1937

1492 Ponce de Leon, N. E.   Druid Hills - Atlanta 7, Ga.

An exclusive Club Residence for refined business and professional girls — permanent guests

Located in one of Atlanta's best residential sections

An address that any young business lady should be proud of — and feel free and at ease in an atmosphere of dignity and refinement

This Foursquare house was originally the home of R.N. Fickett, an illustrious potentate at the Yaarab temple. His wealth came from his broom and mop company. It changed hands many times during the years, each time becoming more and more dilapidated. Finally, it was left open, and a man was murdered inside. In 2018, the home was purchased and is in the process of being completely renovated. (Courtesy of Sue Sullivan.)

This is a photograph of the Hicks house, which had eight bedrooms, each with 18-inch-thick walls of Stone Mountain granite. It was built in 1852. It had a barn with stalls for eight horses, and the original house sat on 50 acres of land. The house was on Williams Mill Road, now known as Briarcliff Road near the intersection of the By Way. Williams Mill, at the time, was a street of many dairies. (Courtesy of Sue Sullivan.)

The International Society for Krishna Consciousness (ISKCON) purchased three dilapidated homes on Ponce de Leon in the 1970s. Two of the houses are used for members of Hare Krishna, who live on the property. One house is a temple, and one is occupied by their "sacred plant."

Eight

DRUID HILLS FIGHTS AN EXPRESSWAY

In 1957, a Stone Mountain Expressway was proposed to connect downtown Atlanta with communities east of Atlanta. It was touted as a commuter road for suburbanites. In 1961, plans for the highway were presented to the Atlanta Region Planning Commission. It was necessary to acquire homes, businesses, and land to build the road. In 1966, work began on the expressway closest to Stone Mountain and downtown Atlanta. The Georgia Department of Transportation (GADOT) plan was to connect these two expressway stubs. By 1966, the government required environmental impact statements for road projects. By 1972, it was decided to put the road on hold until the public transit system opened. In 1974, Atlanta mayor Maynard Jackson proposed a "Great Museum Park" for the vacant land. Several groups made proposals for what to do with the land. In 1978, the GADOT recommended a four-lane limited-access highway following the old Stone Mountain Expressway route. Others submitted plans that included housing, businesses, and trails, but the GADOT continued to push for a highway.

Former president Jimmy Carter's board chose a 30-acre site for Carter's presidential library within the Great Park on Copinhill, a slight rise where General Sherman had watched the burning of Atlanta.

The GADOT proposed an expressway to access the Carter Library and then extended that expressway to connect with the stub in Stone Mountain. On July 6, 1982, Atlanta City Council voted 11-8 in favor of constructing the highway. This favorable vote followed intense lobbying by President Carter and Mayor Andrew Young.

The expressway split into two segments going north and south of the Carter Library site and bisected Olmsted's historic linear park. In 1982, a coalition of neighborhoods opposing the road formed CAUTION; in 1983, the Olmsted Parks Society was formed. In 1985, a civil disobedience group, Roadbusters, was formed. All three groups fought the road.

Meanwhile, library plans progressed. Carter's organization stated the library could not be built without the expressway, but ground was broken for the library in 1983, and its dedication took place in 1987. Ultimately, the Presidential Parkway was defeated at every level: through the courts, by citizen education, by historic preservationists, peaceful non-cooperative protest, and by common sense. It was a win for Druid Hills and the Olmsted Linear Park. Today, a short piece of the road is all that was built, and in 2018, it was renamed the John Lewis Freedom Parkway in honor of Lewis, a member of the House of Representatives, who lent much opposition to the road.

In a series of legal battles that required hundreds of thousands of monetary donations and nearly 10 years, the road was ultimately defeated in 1992 by an order from Hon. Judge Clarence Seeliger.

A tent city was erected in Shady Side Park right at the point where the proposed expressway was to cross it. Protesters lived in the tents at night and demonstrated during the day along busy Ponce de Leon Avenue.

A huge rally of protest against the expressway was held in Dellwood Park. Here, the crowd listens to speeches denouncing the proposed Presidential Parkway. An honorable representative from Georgia to the House of Representatives, John Lewis gave a rousing speech at the event to the acclaim of everyone at the rally.

Feature writer J.J. Williams of the *BOND Community Star* newspaper set up a booth at the protest rally in Dellwood Park. Some of the posters read, "Stop the Road," and "Road Spells Defeat," for several politicians who supported the road. Here, Williams hands out protest flyers.

To protest the GADOT's plan to bisect Olmsted's Shady Side Park with an expressway, several protesters climbed trees or chained themselves to trees. Police and fire vehicles and personnel were sent to remove the tree climbers. Some protesters were arrested at this and other demonstrations.

Protesters of the Presidential Parkway picket along Ponce de Leon. "Stop the Road" was one slogan. "Olmsted Park, Built 1893, Destroyed ????" was another.

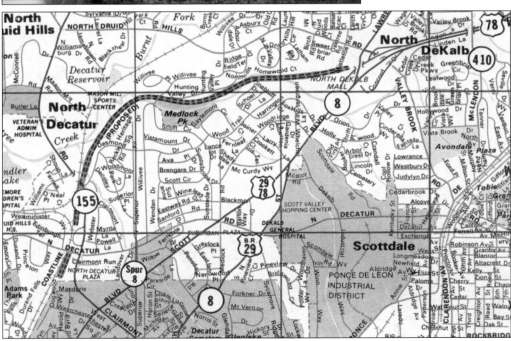

This map of Atlanta shows the route of the Stone Mountain Expressway (also known as the Presidential Parkway and John Lewis Freedom Parkway) as proposed by the Georgia Department of Transportation. The route of the road is shown in the dotted lines on the map and goes through many in-town and historic neighborhoods.

Sally Harbaugh (left) and Tally Sweat sit on an iron bench in Oak Grove Park. Harbaugh did massive research on the Olmsted firm and introduced Druid Hills to his work to the point where Olmsted is now a household name. Harbaugh, who lived in a home overlooking Dellwood Park, had a dream to see the park renovated to how it looked in 1905. Sweat was the first president of Olmsted Linear Park Alliance and was able to raise $10 million to restore the park. Harbaugh had the dream, but Sweat raised the money to pay for it.

Hon. Judge Clarence Seeliger received an award from Olmsted Linear Park Alliance (OLPA) for his order that stopped the road. His 1992 order brought about a settlement agreement between many neighborhoods and organizations and the GADOT. The expressway was not built through Druid Hills. From left to right, Lynn Kerpel, Gale Waldorff, Jennie Richardson, Julie Ralston, Judge Seeliger, Gwin Seeliger, Elana Parent, and Briley Brisendine pose as the judge holds his award.

Emory Village is shown in an aerial view as it looks today. It has changed since first built but remains a vibrant community. (Courtesy of Sue Sullivan.)

This is an aerial shot of Druid Hills as it looks today. It has adhered to the original Olmsted plan for the area and retains the vision for what Olmsted wanted in his design. (Courtesy of Sue Sullivan.)

Druid Hills Today

There is no other completed residential community designed by Frederick Law Olmsted Sr. south of Biltmore Estate in Asheville, North Carolina, except for the linear park and neighborhood in Druid Hills. The late Sally Harbaugh talked about the vistas that beckoned a person to walk forward and observe the beauty of nature. The late Dr. Dana White spoke of "a painting—but with landscape, trees and plants instead of paint." An honorable representative to US Congress, John Lewis said the following at a rally of protesters opposing the Presidential Parkway: "We are standing up for the best of the American tradition." Then Lewis began to chant, "This land is your land; this land is my land; this is not the land of Atlanta City Council or Jimmy Carter or Andrew Young or Tom Moreland! This land is your land! This land is my land!" Lewis received massive applause for his speech. Today, the Presidential Parkway is not completed through Druid Hills. In-town neighborhoods were saved from the expressway. The road was re-named Freedom Parkway and, in 2018, was renamed again the John Lewis Freedom Parkway—a fitting tribute for all Lewis did to stop the road.

For over 100 years, residents of Druid Hills have designed, built, protected, and preserved their unique community. The Olmsted Linear Park Alliance renovated Olmsted's park to its 1905 glory, and to many, it is an honor to live in a place designed by such an artist and genius. Druid Hills was and remains a place worth fighting for, whether against an unnecessary expressway or in the service of historic preservation. Architecture writer and critic Ada Louise Huxtable once said, "And we will probably be judged not by the monuments we build but by those we have destroyed." For now, Druid Hills has been preserved—and the cost is, and will continue to be, eternal vigilance.

Discover Thousands of Local History Books Featuring Millions of Vintage Images

Arcadia Publishing, the leading local history publisher in the United States, is committed to making history accessible and meaningful through publishing books that celebrate and preserve the heritage of America's people and places.

Find more books like this at
www.arcadiapublishing.com

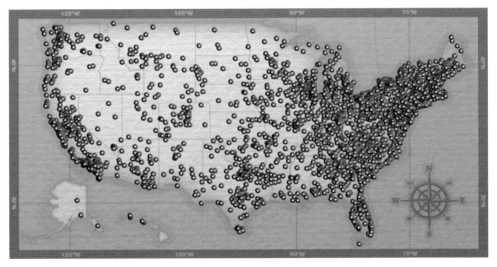

Search for your hometown history, your old stomping grounds, and even your favorite sports team.

Consistent with our mission to preserve history on a local level, this book was printed in South Carolina on American-made paper and manufactured entirely in the United States. Products carrying the accredited Forest Stewardship Council (FSC) label are printed on 100 percent FSC-certified paper.

MADE IN THE USA